Emeril's Cooking
with Power

Also by
Emeril Lagasse

Emeril's Cooking *with* Power

100 DELICIOUS RECIPES STARRING YOUR **SLOW COOKER**, **MULTI-COOKER**, **PRESSURE COOKER**, AND **DEEP FRYER**

Food photography by Colin Lacy

Lifestyle photography by Chris Granger

WM

WILLIAM MORROW

An Imprint of HarperCollins*Publishers*

HarperCollins books may be purchased for educational, business, or sales promotional use. For information please write: Special Markets Department, HarperCollins Publishers, 10 East 53rd Street, New York, NY 10022.

FIRST EDITION

Designed by Leah Carlson-Stanisic

Food photographs by Colin Lacy

Process photographs by Chris Granger

Library of Congress Cataloging-in-Publication Data has been applied for.

ISBN 978-0-06-174298-9

13 14 15 16 17 ID6/RRD 10 9 8 7 6 5 4 3 2 1

To my culinary dream team,

I'm honored and humbled

by your continued dedication

to cook and create with me.

Thank you for all you do.

Contents

Introduction:
Emeril Goes Electric

Everywhere I go, I run into folks who say, "Emeril, I need some new ideas for my slow cooker." Or "I bought a deep fryer but I'm tired of the same old French fries. Can't you help me?" Then there's "What else can you cook in a rice/multi-cooker other than rice?" Or "I'm scared of my pressure cooker. Do you have some recipes that will help me get used to it and also create delicious meals for my family?" It has become a common theme: folks buy electric products to help them manage their time and cooking space better, but then they run out of ideas for new, exciting recipes.

Well, you know I'm a guy who likes to make people happy. So I've put my nose to the grindstone with this one and worked hard to come up with this collection of varied, approachable, and surprising recipes for four of the most commonly found kitchen electrics. Whether you've fallen out of love with your fryer, have a panic attack when attempting to use your pressure cooker, are tired of the same old, same old when you see your slow cooker on the shelf, or have recently acquired a multi-cooker and have no idea how or why to use it, I have assembled more than 100 recipes here for you to renew your connection (no pun intended) with your kitchen electrics.

Set It and Forget It!
Whereas many suburban and rural Americans have enjoyed an affair with their slow cookers for years, it's only recently that they have enjoyed increased popularity in urban settings as well. I am certain that this is due in large part to busier lives, longer workdays, and the fact that in most families today, at least two adults are working full-time. Gone are the days when most households included a member who stayed home to cook, clean, and generally take care of business while the kids were at school and another person worked to bring home the bacon.

Slow cookers make wonderful kitchen helpers in that you can "set it and forget it" and return hours later to a slowly cooked meal just waiting to be served up. The problem is that everyone knows how to do pot roast in a slow cooker, but what about Pot Roast Dianne? Or Artichokes à la Barigoule? Even risotto!

Multi What? The multi-cooker is a relative newcomer to the land of kitchen electrics, but for those of you familiar with the superb results obtained when cooking rice in a rice cooker, the multi-cooker will blow you away. The Emeril by T-fal Multi-Cooker is a remarkable vessel in that it functions as a rice cooker, steamer, and slow cooker all in one, and you can sauté right in the bowl. Some multi-cookers also have roasting programs. So, you can see that for folks with limited kitchen storage space, the multi-cooker can be the way to go. Hey, you'll be amazed at what you can make—anything from a simple stir-fry to a cheesecake! Vegetable dishes, such as Creamed Spinach, Brussels Sprouts Amandine, and Wilted Escarole with Garlic and Crushed Red Pepper, are a breeze in the multi-cooker. Main courses, such as Pork Tenderloin with Spaghetti Squash, Turkey Meatballs, and Steamed Mussels with Fennel and Hot Italian Sausage, come together in no time. And don't forget dessert! The multi-cooker makes great puddings and stewed fruits—how do S'mores Pudding, Drunken Cherries, or Coconut Cardamom Tapioca sound, just for starters?

So if you're like so many others and are looking for new, approachable, exciting ideas to bring to your family table, take a look inside. Go ahead—form a bond with your electrics by cooking your way through these chapters. My hope is that what you find in these pages will be a springboard from which you can take inspiration and create your own unique recipes. As always, it's all about food of love. Enjoy.

Better Under Pressure? The first commercial home pressure cookers made their debut back in the early 1900s and were very popular in the post–World War II period. Though they've gone in and out of fashion several times since, in recent years we've seen a revival of this incredible time-saving tool. But even though they've been around for some time, and have been updated and made less frightening to use, you might be surprised at how many people are afraid of using pressure cookers.

I'm here to tell you that if you adhere to the manufacturer's directions and make sure that you properly close (and open) your pressure cooker, you'll be astounded at the simplicity and speed at which this product functions. Dried beans can be cooked in as little as 15 minutes! Typically long-braised tough meats can be on the table in 45 minutes to an hour instead of the usual 3 to 4 hours. And don't get me started on vegetables! Large-diced pumpkin cooks in 3 minutes. Most poultry dishes are done in 12 to 15 minutes. It's absolutely incredible. The pressure cooker is an indispensable tool for the busy family.

Fear of Frying! Electric fryers have taken the guesswork out of maintaining proper oil temperature, which is what ensures crisp, greaseless fried foods. Now everyone who owns one can make restaurant-quality fried food in their home kitchens without having to attach a cumbersome thermometer to the side of a pot. When purchasing an electric fryer, there are several key features to look for: a built-in oil filtration system, a timer, and at least several temperature settings. More wattage means quicker heat-up. A removable cover means that you can store the oil in the fryer between uses, and some are even vented for splatter-free frying with the lid on. Also, make sure that you purchase a fryer that is the appropriate size for your needs. While folks who live alone or fry infrequently might be able to get away with a tiny fryer, most families will need a fryer that will hold at least 3 quarts of oil so that they can easily feed the entire family at once.

We tested all of the recipes in the fryer section of this book using the Emeril by T-fal Deep Fryer with Integrated Oil Filtration. If your fryer has slightly different temperature settings, simply select the one that is closest to the one recommended here and use common sense to adjust the cook times slightly.

The Slow Cooker:

Set it and forget it!

Slow-Cooked Barbecued Baby Back Ribs

The Slow Cooker

A Note on Slow Cookers

All the recipes in this chapter were tested in the Emeril Slow Cooker by T-fal. It's a 6-quart slow cooker with a removable ceramic bowl. Although it has several unique features, the recipes here will work in any 6-quart slow cooker—just note that the cook times may need to be adjusted slightly, since every slow cooker has minor variations in temperature settings.

If you don't already own a slow cooker, here are a few things to keep in mind when purchasing one:

➤ Size matters! A 6-quart slow cooker is the perfect size for most families and works great for parties and get-togethers.

➤ Digital timers that count down take the guesswork out of knowing when to check your food or when it may be done.

➤ A see-through lid (preferably one that's dishwasher-safe) is perfect for peeking in on your food while it cooks without having to open the lid.

➤ A removable ceramic cooking bowl makes serving, bringing dishes to parties, and cleanup a breeze.

➤ A slow cooker that automatically switches to a "keep warm" setting when the cooking is complete makes it possible to be away for a long day and yet still come home to a hot meal without worrying about overcooking it.

➤ If you can find a slow cooker that automatically boosts the temperature every time the lid is lifted, in order to maintain cook time and proper cooking temperature, I wholeheartedly recommend it. The Emeril Slow Cooker has this feature—we call it "Automatic Temperature Control Technology"—and it works like a charm.

Chicken Stock

The slow cooker is the perfect vessel for making chicken stock because it cooks low and slow, allowing the flavors to meld together gently. The stock doesn't need to be tended to at all. You can usually buy chicken bones from your local butcher, but if you cannot find any, you can use chicken thighs and wings.

1 large yellow onion, halved
1 carrot, cut into 1-inch pieces
1 rib celery, cut into 1-inch pieces
3 cloves garlic
2 bay leaves
2 sprigs fresh parsley
5 black peppercorns
5 pounds raw chicken bones, including carcass, necks, and feet (no fat or skin, but bits of meat are okay), rinsed thoroughly in cold water
3 quarts water, cold or at room temperature

1. Add all the ingredients to a 6-quart slow cooker.

2. Cook on high for 6 hours or low for 10 hours.

3. Skim the surface of the stock, and then strain the stock through a large fine-mesh sieve into a large stockpot or container (discard the bones and vegetables). Allow the stock to cool thoroughly (see Note). Then cover and refrigerate it overnight.

4. Use a spoon to remove any congealed fat from the surface of the chilled stock, and discard it. Store the stock in the refrigerator for up to 1 week, or freeze it in 2- or 4-cup containers, or in ice-cube trays for use in individual dishes, for up to 1 month.

NOTE: *A good method for cooling stock quickly is to place the stockpot in a sink filled with ice and cold water. Stir the stock intermittently as it cools.*

Basic Beef Stock

Keep your freezer stocked! Homemade beef stock is a rich and delicious addition to all of your favorite sauces, stews, and soups. I like to make several batches at a time and freeze it in quart- and pint-size containers so I can pull out just what I need when I need it.

3 pounds beef bones, sawed by the butcher into 2-inch pieces if possible

2 medium yellow onions, unpeeled, halved

2 carrots, peeled, cut into 1-inch chunks

1 pound beef stew meat

2 ribs celery, cut into thirds

1 clove garlic, unpeeled

5 sprigs fresh parsley

1 bay leaf

6 black peppercorns

3 quarts water

1. Preheat the oven to 400°F.

2. Spread the bones out in a roasting pan and roast for 30 minutes. Add the onions and carrots and roast for 30 minutes more, stirring the meat and vegetables once or twice.

3. Place the roasted bones and vegetables in a 6-quart slow cooker. Add all the remaining ingredients to the slow cooker.

4. Cook on high for 4 hours or on low for 8 hours.

5. Strain the stock through a colander or sieve into a large stockpot or other container, and set it aside to cool (see Note, page 5). Discard the bones and vegetables. Then cover and refrigerate the stock overnight.

6. Remove and discard the fat that has accumulated on the surface of the chilled stock.

7. Store the stock in the refrigerator for up to 1 week, or freeze it in 2- or 4-cup containers, or in ice-cube trays for use in individual dishes, for up to 1 month.

Rustic Tomato Soup with Basil Oil and Croustades

There is a wonderful tomato-bread soup made in Tuscany called *pappa al pomodoro*. This is my version, which simmers away in a slow cooker while you crisp bite-size pieces of crusty Italian bread in the oven and make a quick basil–olive oil puree for drizzling. Not exactly like Mama might make it, but wow, this soup could star at your next dinner party.

Tomato soup

2 tablespoons extra-virgin olive oil
3 large yellow onions, sliced lengthwise
    (root to stem) into thin strips
1 tablespoon plus 1 teaspoon kosher salt
¼ teaspoon crushed red pepper
10 cloves garlic, thinly sliced (about ⅓ cup)
Four 28-ounce cans whole San Marzano
    tomatoes, drained, crushed with your hands
8 cups homemade chicken stock (see page 5)
    or packaged low-sodium chicken broth
6 to 8 sprigs fresh thyme
2 large sprigs fresh basil
One 3-inch piece Parmigiano-Reggiano rind

Croustades

8 cups torn bite-size pieces of rustic bread,
    such as ciabatta
2 tablespoons extra-virgin olive oil
Kosher salt
Freshly ground black pepper

Basil oil

¾ cup extra-virgin olive oil
1½ cups packed fresh basil leaves
1 clove garlic, minced
Kosher salt

Shaved Parmigiano-Reggiano cheese,
    for serving
Freshly ground black pepper, for
    serving

1. Start the soup: Heat the olive oil in a large skillet over medium-high heat. When it is hot, add the onions, 1 teaspoon of the salt, and the crushed red pepper. Cook, stirring occasionally, until the onions have softened, about 3 minutes. Add the sliced garlic and continue to cook, stirring, for 3 minutes longer.

2. Transfer the sautéed vegetables to a 6-quart slow cooker and add the tomatoes, chicken stock, thyme and basil sprigs, the remaining 1 tablespoon salt, and the Parmesan rind.

3. Cook on high for 6 hours, stirring occasionally.

4. While the soup is cooking, make the croustades: Preheat the oven to 400°F.

5. Place the torn bread pieces on a large baking sheet and drizzle with the olive oil. Toss with your hands to evenly distribute

the oil. Season lightly with salt and pepper, and bake until golden brown and crisp, 12 to 15 minutes. Set aside to cool.

6. To make the basil oil, combine the olive oil, basil leaves, and minced garlic in a blender or processor. Process in short bursts until the leaves are finely chopped—don't over-process or the leaves will lose their bright green color. Transfer to a small bowl and season to taste with salt.

7. When you are ready to serve the soup, remove and discard the Parmesan rind and thyme sprigs. The basil sprigs should be very soft and can be left in or discarded, as preferred. Taste the soup, and adjust the seasoning if necessary. Ladle the soup into wide shallow bowls and garnish with some of the croustades and Parmesan shavings. Drizzle the basil oil over the soup to taste, and then sprinkle with pepper.

Cuban-Style Slow-Cooked Black Beans

Black beans are hearty enough to stand alone as a main dish, but they also work well in a supporting role alongside other dishes such as roast pork or chicken. Black beans and rice is a staple in many Latin countries and makes for an economical and satisfying meal. If you have any beans left over, use them in quesadillas, burritos, or tacos or add them to your favorite soups and salads.

1 pound dried black beans

4 tablespoons olive oil

1 bay leaf

2 smoked ham hocks

1 large yellow onion, chopped

1½ cups chopped sweet peppers,
    such as Cubanelle, banana, or Italian
    peppers (or substitute bell peppers)

½ cup chopped green onion
    (white and green parts,
    about 3 green onions)

¼ cup chopped seeded jalapeño

3 tablespoons sliced garlic
    (about 5 large cloves)

1 teaspoon dried Mexican oregano or
    regular oregano

1½ teaspoons salt

1 teaspoon freshly ground black pepper

1 teaspoon ground cumin

½ teaspoon ground coriander

3 tablespoons red wine vinegar

⅓ cup dark rum or dry red wine

2 teaspoons sugar

Hot steamed rice, for serving

Finely chopped sweet onion, for garnish

Fresh cilantro leaves, for garnish

1. Soak the beans in water to cover for at least 4 hours and up to overnight.

2. Drain the beans, discard the soaking liquid, and add them to a 6-quart slow cooker along with 6 cups water, 2 tablespoons of the olive oil, and the bay leaf.

3. Cook on high for 4 hours. Then add the ham hocks and cook for another 2 hours.

4. Meanwhile, heat a large sauté pan over medium heat. When it is hot, add the remaining 2 tablespoons olive oil, the onion, sweet peppers, green onion, jalapeño, and garlic and cook for 10 minutes, stirring occasionally. Add the oregano, salt, pepper, cumin, coriander, vinegar, rum, and sugar to the pan and continue to cook until all of the liquid has evaporated, 3 to 4 minutes. Remove from the heat and set aside until ready to use.

5. After the beans have cooked for 6 hours, add the onion mixture to the slow cooker and continue to cook until the beans

are very soft and the cooking liquid has thickened, up to 2½ hours more.

6. When the beans are soft, use a potato masher or the back of a spoon to smash some of the beans, if desired. Remove the bay leaf. Either remove and discard the ham hocks or set them aside to cool, pull the meat from the hocks, and stir the meat into the beans before serving.

7. Serve the black beans with the steamed rice, and garnish with the sweet onion and cilantro.

Artichokes à la Barigoule

This is based on the Provençal dish in which artichokes are braised or stewed in olive oil and white wine. The slow cooker works wonders here, slowly infusing the artichokes with the flavors of lemon, garlic, crushed red pepper, and fresh herbs. Serve these as part of an antipasto platter or as a side dish alongside pasta or pizza.

2¾ cups dry white wine

1¾ cups vegetable oil

1 cup extra-virgin olive oil

½ cup freshly squeezed lemon juice, juiced lemon halves reserved

3 tablespoons kosher salt

1 head garlic, separated into cloves, peeled

4 to 6 sprigs fresh thyme

4 sprigs fresh oregano

1 teaspoon black peppercorns

½ teaspoon crushed red pepper

4 large or 6 medium artichokes

Crusty bread, for serving

1. In a 6-quart slow cooker, combine the wine, vegetable oil, olive oil, lemon juice, 2 of the reserved lemon halves, salt, garlic cloves, thyme and oregano sprigs, peppercorns, and crushed red pepper.

2. Working with one artichoke at a time, and rubbing the cuts with the insides of the remaining lemon halves as you go along, trim a bit off the stem end of the artichokes. Cut off and discard the top third of the artichokes. Pull or trim away any discolored outer leaves. Using kitchen scissors, trim the thorns off the tips of any remaining outer whole leaves. Using a vegetable peeler, peel the tough outer layer of the stems. Cut each trimmed artichoke into quarters, and then cut out and discard the furry choke. As you finish trimming each piece, immediately place it into the wine–olive oil mixture in the slow cooker (this will help prevent discoloration). Once you've finished with all the artichokes, press them into the liquid to submerge them as much as possible.

3. Cook on high for 5 to 6 hours, or until the leaves easily pull away and the hearts are very tender.

4. Serve the artichoke hearts slightly warm or at room temperature, with some of the cooking liquid drizzled over them and crusty bread alongside.

Vegetables à la Grecque

Cooking *à la grecque,* or in the Greek style, simply means slowly cooking vegetables in a braising liquid of olive oil, white wine, lemon juice, and some sort of stock, whether chicken or vegetable, along with herbs and spices. The ingredients list may seem long here, but the steps are fairly simple and the end result is an outstanding dish that can be served as an appetizer or as a side to almost any main.

½ cup olive oil

6 cups quartered assorted mushrooms, wiped clean, and stemmed

2 medium yellow onions, thinly sliced

3 cloves garlic, thinly sliced

About 3 ribs celery, peeled and thinly sliced on the diagonal (2 cups)

About 3 medium carrots, peeled and thinly sliced on the diagonal (2 cups)

About ½ large bulb fennel, core removed, sliced into ¼-inch wedges (2 cups)

2 cups homemade chicken stock (see page 5) or packaged low-sodium chicken broth

½ cup dry white wine

¼ cup freshly squeezed lemon juice

2 teaspoons black peppercorns

3 teaspoons kosher salt, plus more for seasoning

1 teaspoon grated lemon zest

1 teaspoon coriander seeds

½ teaspoon fennel seeds

3 sprigs fresh thyme

1 bay leaf

½ cup torn fresh sorrel leaves (see Note)

2 tablespoons chopped fresh tarragon leaves

1 tablespoon chopped fresh parsley leaves

1. In a large sauté pan, heat 2 tablespoons of the olive oil over medium-high heat. Add the mushrooms, in batches, and sauté them for 3 to 4 minutes, until they are golden brown on both sides.

2. Add the mushrooms, the remaining olive oil, and the remaining ingredients except for the sorrel, tarragon, and parsley to a 6-quart slow cooker.

3. Cook on high for 3 hours, stirring occasionally, until the vegetables are tender and the broth is almost covering them (the vegetables will release their liquid as they cook).

4. Right before serving, remove the bay leaf and stir in the sorrel, tarragon, and parsley, and adjust the seasoning if necessary.

NOTE: *I call for the herb sorrel in this recipe because it adds a tangy element. If you cannot find sorrel, you can substitute spinach or arugula.*

Fire-Roasted Green Chile–Cheese Grits

Green chiles and grits are natural friends. Introduce them to a slab of barbecued ribs and whoa, now there's really a party going on! See for yourself on page 57.

1¼ pounds mixed mild green chiles, such as poblano, Hatch, and/or Anaheim

2 jalapeño or serrano chiles

2 cups old-fashioned grits, such as Quaker (not instant or quick grits)

6 cups water

4 cups whole milk

4 tablespoons (½ stick) unsalted butter

5 teaspoons kosher salt

1 tablespoon minced garlic

1 teaspoon chili powder, plus more for sprinkling if desired

4 ounces pepper Jack cheese, coarsely grated, plus more for garnish

2 ounces sharp yellow cheddar cheese, coarsely grated, plus more for garnish

2 ounces Cotija cheese, crumbled, for garnish

1. Roast all the chiles over an open flame on your cooktop, placing them directly on top of the cooking grates, and allow them to blister and blacken on all sides, turning them with tongs as necessary, 6 to 7 minutes (see Note). Transfer the chiles to a paper bag, crimp the edges closed, and allow them to steam until their skins are loosened and the chiles have cooled slightly, 10 to 15 minutes. Remove the chiles and wipe off the charred skins. Discard the stems and seeds. Chop the chiles and add them to a 6-quart slow cooker along with the grits, water, milk, butter, salt, garlic, and chili powder.

2. Cook on low for 7 hours or on high for 4 hours, whisking occasionally, until the grits are very tender and creamy.

3. Add the 4 ounces pepper Jack and 2 ounces cheddar, and stir until melted. Serve the grits garnished with additional pepper Jack and cheddar, the Cotija, and a sprinkling of chili powder if desired.

NOTE: *Alternatively, if you do not own a gas cooktop, you can blacken the peppers on a grill or rub them with a bit of oil and blister the skins under the broiler.*

Risotto Milanese

Though this is delicious even in its simplicity, I give it distinction with a sprinkling of truffle salt. Truffle butter would also take this dish over the top; use it in place of the 2 tablespoons of butter at the end. You can also use this basic technique to try all varieties of risotto in your slow cooker. Want mushroom risotto? Sauté the mushrooms with the onion and eliminate the saffron. Easy.

5 tablespoons unsalted butter

1½ cups chopped yellow onion

2 teaspoons minced garlic

¼ teaspoon saffron threads

1½ teaspoons salt

¾ teaspoon freshly ground black pepper

2 cups Arborio rice

1 cup dry white wine

5½ cups homemade chicken stock
(see page 5) or packaged
low-sodium chicken broth

1 cup finely grated Parmigiano-Reggiano
cheese, plus more for garnish

Truffle salt, for garnish (see Note)

1. Melt 3 tablespoons of the butter in a 12-inch skillet over medium-high heat. Add the onion and cook for 2 minutes, until softened. Then add the garlic, saffron, salt, and pepper, and toast the saffron for 30 seconds. Stir in the rice and continue to cook, stirring frequently, until the rice is translucent, about 3 minutes. Stir in the wine, reduce the heat to medium, and simmer for 2 minutes, or until the wine has evaporated. Transfer the rice mixture to a 6-quart slow cooker and add the chicken stock.

2. Cook on high for 2 hours.

3. Stir in the remaining 2 tablespoons butter and the 1 cup of Parmesan. Serve warm in bowls, garnished with additional Parmesan and truffle salt.

NOTE: *Truffle salt can be found in gourmet food markets, in some upscale grocery stores, and online. While it's not absolutely necessary here, it adds a complex, earthy note to the risotto. If you cannot find it, simply substitute sea salt or kosher salt.*

Slow-Cooked Potatoes with Mushrooms and Ham

If you're looking for a casserole to die for, it's right here, buddy! Potatoes slow-cooked with cheese and soaked in cream. It doesn't get any better than this—and don't say I didn't warn you.

4 tablespoons (½ stick) unsalted butter

1 cup chopped yellow onion (about 1 medium onion)

1 pound button or shiitake mushrooms, or a mix of your favorite mushrooms, wiped clean, stemmed, and sliced

1 tablespoon chopped garlic (2 to 3 cloves)

1½ teapoons salt

1½ teaspoons freshly ground black pepper

4 pounds Idaho potatoes, peeled and submerged in a bowl of water

8 ounces thinly sliced Black Forest ham

4 ounces Gruyère cheese, grated

1 cup homemade chicken stock (see page 5) or packaged low-sodium chicken broth

3 sprigs fresh thyme, plus 1 tablespoon fresh thyme leaves

1 cup heavy cream

1. Melt the butter in a 12-inch skillet over medium-high heat. Add the onion and cook for 1 minute. Add the mushrooms, raise the heat to high, and continue cooking, stirring as needed, for 5 minutes. Add the garlic, ½ teaspoon of the salt, and ½ teaspoon of the pepper. Remove from the heat and set aside.

2. Generously coat a 6-quart slow cooker with cooking spray. Slice half of the potatoes into ⅛-inch-thick slices on a mandoline. Shingle the potatoes in two layers in the slow cooker, and season them with ½ teaspoon of the salt and ½ teaspoon of the pepper. Top the potatoes with half of the mushroom-onion mixture and gently spread it out in an even layer. Arrange half of the ham slices over the potatoes, top with half of the Gruyère, and pour in half of the chicken stock. Repeat with the remaining potatoes, salt, pepper, mushroom mixture, and ham. Add the remaining ½ cup chicken stock. Using a metal spatula, gently press the ingredients so the layers are even. Tuck the thyme sprigs around the edges.

3. Cook on high for 4 hours, or until the potatoes are tender. You can test for doneness by inserting the blade of a thin knife into the center. There should be little resistance.

4. Drizzle in the heavy cream and cook for another 30 minutes.

5. When the casserole is done, top it with the remaining Gruyère and the fresh thyme leaves. Turn off the cooker. Allow the potatoes to cool enough to set before serving, about 1 hour, covered.

Sicilian Eggplant

My friends in Sicily really know how to cook eggplant. They often prepare it very simply—grilled, drizzled with olive oil, and garnished with chopped mint and basil. Here I take it a step or two further and marry all those flavors together with tomatoes, two Italian cheeses, and just enough breadcrumbs to bind it all. The result is a vegetarian casserole that is reminiscent of the best that eggplant Parmesan has to offer, and then some.

3 pounds Italian eggplants (3 large)

3½ teaspoons kosher salt

6 tablespoons extra-virgin olive oil

⅓ cup minced garlic (about 10 large cloves)

2 teaspoons minced canned anchovy fillets (4 to 6 fillets)

1 teaspoon crushed red pepper

Three 28-ounce cans Italian-style whole peeled tomatoes, drained, crushed with your hands

One 28-ounce can tomato sauce

3 tablespoons nonpareil capers, plus 1 tablespoon caper liquid

9 tablespoons fresh breadcrumbs

8 ounces sliced provolone cheese

10 ounces part-skim mozzarella cheese, coarsely grated

3 tablespoons chopped fresh mint leaves

3 tablespoons chopped fresh basil leaves, plus ¼ cup chiffonade for garnish

Crusty bread, for serving

1. Slice the eggplants crosswise into ⅓-inch-thick rounds. Place the eggplant slices in a single layer on paper towels, and sprinkle on both sides with 2 teaspoons of the salt. Let sit for at least 30 minutes and up to 1 hour; then pat dry with paper towels.

2. Position an oven rack 6 to 8 inches from the broiler unit, and preheat the broiler to high.

3. Transfer the eggplant slices to two large baking sheets, and brush the tops of the slices with 3 tablespoons of the olive oil. Broil until softened and lightly golden, about 6 minutes. Set aside.

4. In a very large skillet, heat the remaining 3 tablespoons olive oil over medium-high heat. When it is hot, add the garlic, anchovies, and crushed red pepper and cook, stirring, until fragrant, 1 minute. Do not allow the garlic to brown. Add the tomatoes, tomato sauce, capers, caper liquid, and remaining 1½ teaspoons salt, and raise the heat to high. Cook, stirring occasionally, until the sauce is very thick, 15 minutes.

5. Sprinkle the bottom of a 6-quart slow cooker with 3 tablespoons of the breadcrumbs, and layer one-third of the eggplant slices over the crumbs. Spread 2 cups of the tomato sauce over the eggplant, and then top it with half of the sliced provolone, ⅓ cup of the mozzarella, and 1 tablespoon each of the chopped mint and basil. Repeat with another layer of breadcrumbs, half of the remaining eggplant, another 2 cups of sauce, the remaining provolone, ⅓ cup of the mozzarella, and 1 tablespoon each of the herbs. Repeat a final time with the remaining breadcrumbs, the remaining eggplant, remaining sauce, and remaining herbs, and then top with the remaining mozzarella.

6. Cook on high for 2 hours.

7. Let rest for at least 15 minutes before serving. Garnish with the chiffonade of basil and serve with crusty bread.

Linguine with Clam Sauce

One of my favorite classics, prepared in an unconventional way. You start the sauce on the stove, then transfer it to the slow cooker and walk away. For 3 hours! Nothing to worry about. Enjoy it with crusty bread and a green salad.

4 tablespoons (½ stick) unsalted butter

¼ cup chopped bacon (about 2 strips)

1 cup chopped yellow onion
    (about 1 medium onion)

½ cup chopped shallot (about 2 medium
    shallots)

¼ cup minced garlic (about 8 large cloves)

¼ teaspoon crushed red pepper

1 teaspoon salt

4 large canned anchovy fillets (see Note)

¼ cup all-purpose flour

1 cup dry white wine

1 cup bottled clam juice

Two 6.5-ounce cans minced clams,
    with juices

Two 10-ounce cans whole baby clams,
    with juices

1 pound linguine, spaghetti, or fettuccine

¼ cup chopped fresh parsley leaves

½ cup finely grated Parmigiano-Reggiano
    cheese, plus more for serving

Freshly ground white pepper, for garnish
    (optional)

Extra-virgin olive oil, for garnish (optional)

1. Melt the butter in a 12-inch skillet over medium-high heat. Add the bacon and cook until the fat is rendered, about 3 minutes. Add the onion, shallot, garlic, crushed red pepper, salt, and anchovies, and cook for 3 minutes longer. Stir in the flour and continue to cook for another 5 minutes. Whisk in the wine, bring to a simmer, and then transfer the mixture to a 6-quart slow cooker. Add the clam juice and clams.

2. Cook on high for 3 hours.

3. When you're ready to eat, cook the linguine in boiling salted water until al dente according to the package directions. Drain the pasta, and add it to the slow cooker. Allow it to sit in the sauce on the warm setting for at least 5 minutes before serving. (As the pasta sits in the sauce, the sauce will thicken and coat the noodles.) Right before serving, stir in the parsley and Parmesan.

4. Serve with additional Parmesan, a sprinkling of white pepper, and a drizzle of olive oil if desired.

NOTE: *It's not necessary to chop the anchovies; they will break into small pieces while cooking.*

Shrimp and Lima Beans

Classic Southern fare made easy in the slow cooker. Instead of having to have shrimp stock on hand, I chop some of the shrimp and bacon, add it to the pot with the beans, and allow it all to simmer ever so slowly to impart deep flavor. Whole shrimp is stirred in at the end and the dish is topped off with crisped bacon.

1½ pounds shrimp, peeled and deveined

6 strips bacon

1 pound dried large lima beans, or baby limas if preferred

1 cup chopped yellow onion (about 1 medium onion)

½ cup chopped celery (about 1 rib)

5 cloves garlic, smashed

1 tablespoon tomato paste

2 bay leaves

1 tablespoon Creole Seasoning (recipe follows) or Emeril's Original Essence

1½ teaspoons salt

2 sprigs fresh thyme, or 1 teaspoon dried thyme

½ teaspoon crushed red pepper, plus more for garnish

6 cups water

¼ cup chopped fresh parsley leaves, plus more for garnish

Hot steamed rice, for serving

1. Chop half of the shrimp and add them to a 6-quart slow cooker. Cover and refrigerate the remaining shrimp. Chop 2 strips of the bacon and add them to the slow cooker, along with the beans, onion, celery, garlic, tomato paste, bay leaves, Creole Seasoning, salt, thyme, crushed red pepper, and water.

2. Cook on high for 4 hours.

3. While the shrimp and lima beans are cooking, chop the remaining 4 strips bacon and cook it in a small skillet over medium heat until the fat is rendered and the bacon is crispy, about 5 minutes. Remove the bacon with a slotted spoon and set it aside on paper towels to drain.

4. During the last 5 minutes of cooking, stir the reserved shrimp and the ¼ cup chopped parsley into the slow cooker.

5. Remove and discard the bay leaves, and the thyme sprigs if using. Serve the shrimp and lima beans in bowls, spooned over steamed rice and garnished with the crisped bacon. Top with additional crushed red pepper and parsley as desired.

Creole Seasoning ⅔ cup

2½ tablespoons paprika

2 tablespoons salt

2 tablespoons garlic powder

1 tablespoon freshly ground black pepper

1 tablespoon onion powder

1 tablespoon cayenne pepper

1 tablespoon dried oregano

1 tablespoon dried thyme

Combine all the ingredients thoroughly and store in an airtight container for up to 1 year.

Crawfish Étouffée

Make sure you purchase Louisiana crawfish tails for this dish—the flavor of the imported variety pales when compared to our local crustaceans. Your seafood monger should be able to order some for you if you can't find them easily where you live. If you have a group coming for dinner, this can easily be prepared a day or two in advance and then slowly reheated just before serving. All you need to serve with this indulgent dish is a green salad and some crusty French bread, and then *laissez les bons temps rouler!*

8 tablespoons (1 stick) unsalted butter

½ cup plus 2 tablespoons all-purpose flour

4 cups chopped onion (about 3 medium onions)

2 cups chopped celery (3 to 4 ribs)

2 cups chopped green bell pepper (about 1½ medium peppers)

1 bunch green onions, chopped, tops and bottoms reserved separately

2 tablespoons minced garlic (4 to 5 large cloves)

One 14.5-ounce can diced tomatoes, with juices

1½ cups shrimp stock, light fish stock, homemade chicken stock (see page 5), or packaged low-sodium chicken broth

2 tablespoons Creole Seasoning (page 29) or Emeril's Original Essence

1 tablespoon tomato paste

½ teaspoon cayenne pepper

2 teaspoons kosher salt, plus more to taste

Two 1-pound packages peeled Louisiana crawfish tails, with any fat

Hot steamed white rice, for serving

¼ cup chopped fresh parsley leaves, for garnish

Louisiana hot sauce, for serving

1. Melt the butter in a large Dutch oven over medium-high heat. Whisk in the flour and cook, stirring constantly and scraping all parts of the bottom of the pot, until a peanut-butter-colored roux is formed, about 8 minutes. Immediately add the onion, celery, bell pepper, and green onion bottoms, and cook, stirring frequently, until the vegetables have softened, about 6 minutes. Add the garlic and cook for 1 to 2 minutes more. Then stir in the tomatoes and their juices, shrimp stock, Creole Seasoning, tomato paste, cayenne pepper, and the 2 teaspoons salt. Once the mixture comes to a boil, transfer it to a 6-quart slow cooker.

2. Cook on low for 6 hours or on high for 4 hours, until the sauce is velvety and smooth and without a trace of flouriness. Thirty minutes before the cooking is complete, stir in the crawfish and the green onion tops.

3. Taste, and adjust the seasoning if necessary. Serve over steamed white rice in wide, shallow bowls, garnished with the parsley. Pass the hot sauce at the table for guests to use to their liking.

Stuffed Calamari in a Smoky Tomato Sauce

6 servings

This dish was developed for the Feast of the Seven Fishes, an Italian Christmas Eve tradition at which seven courses of fish are served. The squid are stuffed with a mixture of sausage, shrimp, and squid and then slowly braised in a light tomato sauce spiked with hot pimentón. Try to buy fairly large squid—it makes stuffing them slightly easier.

2 tablespoons olive oil

6 ounces mild fresh Italian sausage, in bulk or removed from casings

½ cup minced shallot (about 2 medium shallots)

2 cloves garlic, minced

1 teaspoon sea salt

1 pound fresh squid (you will need about 36 bodies)

6 ounces shrimp, peeled, deveined, and finely chopped

½ cup fresh breadcrumbs

2 tablespoons finely grated Parmigiano-Reggiano cheese

2 tablespoons whole milk

1 tablespoon chopped fresh parsley leaves

1 tablespoon chopped fresh basil leaves

½ teaspoon crushed red pepper

2 cups Smoky Tomato Sauce (recipe follows)

1. Preheat the oven to 400°F.

2. Heat the olive oil in a 12-inch sauté pan over medium-high heat. Add the sausage and cook for 2 minutes, or just until browned. Using a slotted spoon, transfer the sausage to a large mixing bowl. Reduce the heat to medium, add the shallot to the pan, and cook until it is softened but not browned, about 2 minutes. Add the garlic and salt, and cook until fragrant, 30 seconds to 1 minute. Transfer the shallot mixture to the bowl containing the sausage. Set aside to cool.

3. To thoroughly clean the squid, cut the bodies from the tentacles and turn the bodies inside out. Rinse the bodies and the tentacles under cool running water. Use paper towels to pat dry. Place the bodies on a baking sheet or in a bowl, and refrigerate, covered, until ready to use. Finely chop the tentacles so that there aren't any large pieces. Transfer the tentacles to the bowl containing the sausage. Add the shrimp, breadcrumbs, Parmesan, milk, parsley, basil, and crushed red pepper. Stir well to combine.

4. Remove the squid bodies from the refrigerator, and using a small spoon or your hands, carefully stuff the bodies with the filling, dividing the mixture evenly

among them. Do not overstuff the squid—
the stuffing expands somewhat as it cooks.

5. Place the stuffed squid in a 6-quart slow
cooker and spoon the Smoky Tomato Sauce
over them.

6. Cook on high for 1 hour.

7. Serve immediately.

Smoky Tomato Sauce   3 cups

This sauce is terrific on pasta, and makes a
great dipping sauce for fried mozzarella or
calamari.

2 tablespoons unsalted butter
3 cloves garlic, sliced
1 small yellow onion, finely diced
2 bay leaves
½ teaspoon crushed red pepper
½ teaspoon pimentón picante (hot smoked
    Spanish paprika)
2½ pounds ripe tomatoes, peeled, seeded, and
    chopped
2 tablespoons olive oil
1 teaspoon salt
½ teaspoon freshly ground black pepper

1. In a medium saucepan over medium heat,
melt the butter. Add the garlic, onion, bay
leaves, crushed red pepper, and pimentón
and cook until the onion has softened, 2 to 3
minutes. Add the tomatoes (and any juices)
to the saucepan.

2. Cook over medium heat, stirring
occasionally, until the mixture is very thick.

3. Cool the tomato sauce briefly, and remove
the bay leaves. Then puree it in a blender
along with the olive oil, salt, and black
pepper (in batches if necessary) until very
smooth (see Note).

4. Use the sauce as desired or store it in
a covered nonreactive container in the
refrigerator for up to 1 week or in the freezer
for up to several months.

NOTE: *Please use caution when blending
hot liquids: blend only small amounts at a
time, with the blender tightly covered and
a kitchen towel held over the top.*

Colombian Chicken, Corn, and Potato Stew

Ajiaco, pronounced *ah-hee-a-ko,* is a classic stew from Colombia that highlights that country's prized creamy native potatoes, its native herb *guascas* (an herbaceous plant with a flavor close to a mixture of parsley and bay leaf, with perhaps a bit of oregano—it's difficult to describe), and its native large-kernel corn. But, hey, that doesn't stop me from enjoying some in my own home. In my own slow cooker, no doubt! This is a great example of a stew where you can pile in all the fresh ingredients and just let it go.

3½ to 4 pounds whole chicken legs
   (drumstick and thigh)
2 tablespoons salt
1½ teaspoons freshly ground black pepper,
   plus more as needed
3 tablespoons unsalted butter
1 yellow onion, chopped
1 serrano chile or 2 jalapeños,
   stemmed, seeded, and chopped
1 teaspoon dried oregano
1 bay leaf
1 pound russet potatoes, peeled and cut into
   ½-inch cubes
1 pound Yukon Gold potatoes,
   peeled and cut into 1-inch cubes
1 pound Red Bliss potatoes, halved and
   quartered

3 ears sweet corn, broken in half,
   or 3 cups thawed frozen corn kernels
   (see Notes)
7 cups homemade chicken stock
   (see page 5) or packaged low-sodium
   chicken broth
¼ cup nonpareil capers,
   drained and chopped
½ cup chopped fresh cilantro leaves
½ cup chopped fresh parsley leaves
3 avocados, for serving
3 limes, cut into wedges, for serving
Mexican crema (see Notes), crème fraîche,
   or sour cream, for serving

1. Season the chicken all over with 1 tablespoon of the salt and the 1½ teaspoons pepper. Melt the butter in a large sauté pan over medium heat, and cook the chicken, in batches, until nicely browned on both sides, about 10 minutes. Transfer the chicken to a 6-quart slow cooker.

2. Add the onion, serrano chile, oregano, bay leaf, potatoes, corn on the cob (if using), chicken stock, and the remaining 1 tablespoon salt.

3. Cook on low for 5 hours. After 4 hours of cooking, transfer the chicken and corn to a platter and set aside until cool enough to handle. Meanwhile, using a potato masher or a whisk, break apart one-third to one-

half of the potato chunks in the cooker to thicken the stew.

4. Once the chicken is cool enough to handle, discard the skin and bones, shred the meat, and return it to the slow cooker.

5. Once the corn is cool enough to handle, cut the kernels from the cobs and return them to the slow cooker. Discard the cobs.

6. Right before serving, stir in the capers, cilantro, and parsley. Peel, seed, and chop the avocados, and squeeze some of the lime over them to prevent discoloration. Serve the stew in bowls, garnished with the avocado, remaining lime wedges, crema, and additional black pepper as desired.

NOTES: *If you substitute frozen corn kernels for the corn on the cob, add them to the slow cooker along with the shredded chicken during the last hour of cooking.*

If you are able to find guascas *in a Latin market, use ¼ cup in place of the bay leaf and oregano.*

Mexican crema, though similar to crème fraîche, is thinner in consistency. It can be found in Latin markets and sometimes in the dairy section of mainstream grocery stores.

Seafood and Smoked Sausage Gumbo

8 servings

With this recipe you might be able to argue that you don't need a gumbo pot. To keep your doubters at bay, transfer the finished slow-cooker gumbo to your favorite pot and set it on the stove. No one will ever know you didn't sweat over it all day.

1 cup vegetable oil

1½ cups all-purpose flour

2½ cups chopped onion
    (about 2 medium onions)

1½ cups chopped celery
    (about 3 ribs)

1½ cups chopped green bell pepper
    (about 1 medium pepper)

2 tablespoons chopped garlic
    (4 to 5 large cloves)

1 teaspoon Creole Seasoning (page 29)
    or Emeril's Original Essence

1½ teaspoons salt

1 teaspoon freshly ground black pepper

½ teaspoon cayenne pepper

2 bay leaves

1 teaspoon dried thyme

1 teaspoon dried oregano

1 pound smoked sausage,
    cut into ½-inch-thick rounds

1 pound gumbo crabs (see Note),
    halved

6 cups water

1 pound peeled Louisiana crawfish tails

1 pound shrimp, peeled and deveined

½ cup chopped green onion,
    plus more for serving

¼ cup chopped fresh parsley leaves,
    plus more for serving

Hot steamed white rice, for serving

1. Heat a 14-inch heavy-bottomed skillet or Dutch oven over high heat for 1 minute. Carefully pour in the oil and then whisk in the flour. Reduce the heat to medium-high and stir the flour constantly for 15 minutes, until evenly browned. It should be the color of peanut butter. If you find the flour is coloring too fast, reduce the heat to medium. It is important to watch the roux and cook it carefully to avoid burning. Once the desired color is reached, add the onion, celery, bell pepper, garlic, Creole Seasoning, salt, black pepper, cayenne, bay leaves, thyme, oregano, and sausage. Cook for 5 minutes, and then remove from the heat.

2. Transfer the mixture to a 6-quart slow cooker. Add the crabs and the water.

3. Cook on high for 5 hours. Then stir in the crawfish and shrimp, and cook for another 30 minutes. Remove the bay leaves.

4. Right before serving, stir in the ½ cup green onion and the ¼ cup chopped parsley. Serve the gumbo over bowls of

steamed rice, garnished with additional chopped parsley and green onion as desired.

> NOTE: *Gumbo crabs are blue crabs that are not graded #1, simply because they may not be as heavy (full of crabmeat) as #1-graded crabs. They are kept aside and sold as gumbo crabs for folks to flavor soups and stews, such as this gumbo. You can often find them in the freezer section of grocery stores in Louisiana. If you cannot find them where you live, you can simply substitute 2 regular blue crabs if desired. They are used mostly to flavor the gumbo and are not typically eaten at the table.*

Jerk Chicken with Rice and Peas

Traditional Jamaican jerk is of course slowly cooked over coals to impart smoky flavors and Scotch Bonnet heat. You'll be amazed at how I pull it off here with a fiery-hot marinade and only 5 minutes on the grill.

Note that you will need to start this dish a day in advance, so that the chicken has just the right amount of time to sit in the marinade and soak up all the wonderful jerk seasonings.

Two 3½-pound chickens, backbones removed, cut in half through the breastbone

2 cups distilled white vinegar

9 Scotch Bonnet chiles, stemmed, seeded, and halved

9 cloves garlic

1½ cups chopped green onion (white and green parts, about 1½ bunches)

3 tablespoons light brown sugar

3 bay leaves, crumbled

2¼ teaspoons dried thyme

2½ tablespoons ground allspice

1½ teaspoons ground cinnamon

1 tablespoon freshly ground black pepper

1 tablespoon plus 1½ teaspoons salt

6 tablespoons freshly squeezed lime juice

3 tablespoons soy sauce

2 tablespoons grapeseed or other vegetable oil

Rice and Peas (recipe follows), for serving

1. Place the chicken in a large bowl, add the vinegar, and toss until coated. Transfer the chicken to a large platter or rimmed baking sheet, and discard the vinegar.

2. To make the marinade, combine the chiles, garlic, green onion, brown sugar, bay leaves, thyme, allspice, cinnamon, black pepper, 1 tablespoon of the salt, the lime juice, and soy sauce in a food processor or blender, and process until smooth, about 1 minute. Measure out ⅓ cup plus 1 tablespoon of the marinade and set that aside, covered, in a small container in the refrigerator until ready to serve. Spoon the remaining marinade all over the chicken, and transfer the chicken to a large resealable plastic bag set in a bowl (to catch any leaks), or to a large container and cover it. Refrigerate overnight.

3. Remove the chicken from the marinade and set it on a large platter. Add any marinade that did not adhere to the chicken to a 6-quart slow cooker.

4. Heat a cast-iron grill pan over medium-high heat and brush it with the grapeseed oil. (Alternatively, you can heat an outdoor grill to medium-high and brush the grates with the oil.) Season the chicken all over with the remaining 1½ teaspoons salt. Once the grill pan is hot, cook the chicken,

skin side down, in batches as necessary, for 2 to 3 minutes, or until nicely marked. Turn the chicken over and cook for another 2 to 3 minutes. (This will produce a lot of smoke, so be sure to use your vent hood or fan.) Transfer the chicken to the slow cooker.

5. Cook on low for 4 hours.

6. Carefully remove the chicken from the slow cooker (it will be very tender) and cut each half into 2 pieces. Brush some of the reserved marinade over each piece, and serve with the Rice and Peas alongside and the jus from the slow cooker spooned over all. (Alternatively, after cutting the chicken, you can stir the reserved marinade into the jus, then return the chicken to the pot and allow guests to serve themselves.)

Rice and Peas 8 servings

A coconut creamy accompaniment for Jerk Chicken, or for any other time you just want some good rice.

2 tablespoons vegetable oil
½ cup chopped green onion
    (about 3 green onions)
1 tablespoon minced garlic
    (2 to 3 cloves)
½ teaspoon dried thyme
½ teaspoon salt
½ teaspoon freshly ground black pepper
2 cups long-grain white rice
One 15-ounce can dark red kidney beans,
    rinsed and drained
One 15-ounce can unsweetened coconut milk
2 cups water

Heat the oil in a 2-quart or larger pot set over medium-high heat. Add the green onion, garlic, thyme, salt, and pepper, and cook, stirring frequently, for 1 minute. Stir in the rice and cook, stirring, until the rice is translucent, 1 to 2 minutes. Stir in the beans, coconut milk, and water. Bring the liquid to a simmer, cover the pot, and reduce the heat to low. Cook the rice for 18 minutes. Remove from the heat and fluff with a fork.

Chicken with 40 Cloves of Garlic

In this classic French dish, you will not believe how smooth and mellow the garlic becomes with long, slow cooking. Make it for your next dinner party: brown the chicken, throw the rest of the ingredients into the slow cooker, and leave it alone. Stir in a quick beurre manié at the end and voilà, dinner is served! It's great over cooked white rice or buttered noodles or alongside crusty French bread.

2 tablespoons olive oil

12 bone-in, skin-on chicken thighs (about 4 pounds)

3 teaspoons kosher salt

1¾ teaspoons freshly ground black pepper

2 tablespoons chopped fresh rosemary leaves

Leaves from 6 sprigs fresh thyme (2 teaspoons thyme leaves)

40 cloves garlic, from 2 to 3 heads

1 cup dry white wine

2 tablespoons plus 2 teaspoons freshly squeezed lemon juice, or to taste

3 tablespoons all-purpose flour

2 tablespoons unsalted butter, at room temperature

2 tablespoons chopped fresh parsley leaves

1. Heat a large skillet over medium-high heat, and when it is hot, add the olive oil. Season the chicken on both sides with 2½ teaspoons of the salt and 1½ teaspoons of the pepper. Working in batches so as to not crowd the skillet, sear the chicken, skin side down, until golden brown, about 6 minutes. Brown briefly on the second side, and then transfer the browned chicken to a 6-quart slow cooker. Sprinkle the chicken with the rosemary, thyme leaves, and garlic. Then pour the wine and 2 tablespoons of the lemon juice over the chicken.

2. Cook on low for 4½ hours, rearranging the chicken once or twice to ensure even cooking, until it is fall-off-the-bone tender. Transfer the chicken and some of the garlic cloves to a platter and cover to keep warm.

3. In a medium bowl, stir the flour and butter together to form a smooth paste. Whisk ½ cup of the hot juices from the slow cooker into the flour-butter mixture until smooth. Then add this mixture to the slow cooker and whisk to combine with the remaining juices. Cover and continue to cook until the gravy has thickened, 20 to 30 minutes.

4. Stir in the remaining 2 teaspoons lemon juice, and season the sauce with the remaining ½ teaspoon salt and ¼ teaspoon pepper. Serve the chicken with the gravy spooned over the top and sprinkled with the parsley.

Layered Chicken Enchiladas

A casserole favorite adapted to the slow cooker. You can easily make this with beef or chorizo: brown ground beef seasoned with salt and pepper, or the sausage, in a pan—the most important thing is to render as much fat as possible—and just replace the chicken. Or really change it up and substitute drained canned beans. So versatile!

6 tablespoons vegetable oil

6 tablespoons all-purpose flour

½ cup (about 2 ounces) chili powder

2 teaspoons dried oregano

1 teaspoon ground cumin

½ teaspoon salt

4 cups homemade chicken stock (see page 5) or packaged low-sodium chicken broth

Two 15-ounce cans tomato sauce

4 cups shredded or diced cooked chicken

8 ounces cheddar cheese, shredded

4 ounces Monterey Jack cheese, shredded

1 medium yellow onion, chopped

Sixteen 6-inch corn tortillas

¾ cup crumbled Cotija cheese, for garnish

1 bunch green onions, chopped, for garnish

½ cup chopped fresh cilantro leaves, for garnish

Sour cream, for serving

1. Heat the oil in a 2-quart or larger pot over medium-high heat. Stir in the flour and cook for 1 minute. Stir in the chili powder, oregano, cumin, and salt, and cook for 30 seconds longer. Stir in the chicken stock and tomato sauce and bring to a boil. Reduce the heat to low and simmer for 15 minutes, until the flavors are blended. Set the enchilada sauce aside to cool.

2. In a medium bowl, combine the chicken with the cheddar, Monterey Jack, and chopped onion.

3. Add 1 cup of the enchilada sauce to a 6-quart slow cooker and top it with 4 tortillas (they will slightly overlap). Add 2 cups of the chicken-cheese filling, spreading it evenly, and top with 4 more tortillas. Continue to build two more layers of sauce/filling/tortillas. Top the final layer with 1 cup of the sauce.

4. Cook on high for 2 hours. During the last 10 minutes of cooking, pour another ½ cup of sauce over the top.

5. Shortly before serving, garnish the enchilada with the Cotija, green onions, and cilantro. Allow it to sit for 10 minutes. Then cut it into individual portions and serve with the remaining sauce and the sour cream alongside.

Duck Confit

Duck confit is a French dish made with cured duck legs that are cooked slowly in duck fat. The term *confit* technically means anything cooked in its own fat. Here we take duck legs and cook them in a neutral-flavored oil. It takes a little time and some patience but is *soo* worth it—the duck meat becomes melt-in-your-mouth tender. Your friends will be impressed when you serve this restaurant-style dish at your next dinner party. I suggest serving it as a first course with a simple green salad.

⅓ cup kosher salt

2 tablespoons sugar

3 bay leaves

2 tablespoons fresh thyme leaves

2 tablespoons packed fresh parsley leaves

2 tablespoons minced shallot

2 teaspoons black peppercorns

1 teaspoon fresh oregano leaves

1 teaspoon grated lemon zest

4 whole duck legs (drumstick and thigh)

4 cups canola or grapeseed oil

1. Combine the salt, sugar, bay leaves, thyme, parsley, shallot, peppercorns, oregano, and lemon zest in a small food processor or spice grinder. Process until the mixture is well combined and bright green.

2. Trim off any excess fat or skin from the duck legs. Then rinse and pat them dry. Rub the duck legs with the salt mixture, dividing it evenly among the legs. Place the duck legs, flesh side up, in one layer in a baking dish. Cover and refrigerate for 24 hours to cure.

3. Rinse the duck legs and pat them dry. Place them in a 6-quart slow cooker and add the oil.

4. Cook on low for 4 hours. When the duck is done, it will be very tender and the meat on the drumstick will have shrunk towards the thigh and some of the bone will be exposed. The fat should be clear, indicating that the meat is no longer releasing any juices.

5. Remove the insert from the slow cooker and allow the duck, still in the insert, to cool slowly to room temperature. When the duck has cooled, gently lift the legs out of the fat and transfer them to a container, skin side up. Cover the duck completely with its cooking fat (be careful not to add any of the meat juices), cover the container, and refrigerate until ready to use, up to 1 month. (If you plan to store the confit for any length

of time, it is important to be extremely careful about not getting any meat juices in the container, as that will cause it to spoil.)

6. To serve, remove the duck from the refrigerator and allow it to sit at room temperature for at least 30 minutes so that the fat can soften.

7. Preheat the oven to 375°F.

8. Gently lift the duck legs out of the fat, scraping off any excess. Strain the fat through a colander and save it for another use (see Note). Heat a nonstick or cast-iron skillet over medium-high heat. Add the duck, skin side down, and cook until the skin is golden brown and crisp, 5 to 6 minutes. Transfer the duck legs to a baking dish, skin side up, and bake for 8 minutes to heat them through.

NOTE: *The strained fat can be stored in a resealable container in the refrigerator for up to 3 months. It will have taken on a delicious duck flavor and can be used for deep-frying, pan-frying, or sautéing.*

Slow-Cooked Lasagna

Here's nothing fancy, just awesome lasagna. You can assemble the entire thing the day or night before, then put it in your slow cooker and flip the switch when you're hours away from dinner. A green salad, a loaf of crusty bread, and a good full-bodied red wine are all you need. A dinner with friends, on a weeknight!

Meat sauce

⅓ pound ground beef

⅓ pound ground veal

⅓ pound ground pork

½ cup chopped celery
   (about 1 rib)

1 small yellow onion, chopped

3 tablespoons chopped garlic
   (6 to 7 cloves)

Two 28-ounce cans crushed tomatoes

1 cup homemade beef stock
   (see page 6) or packaged low-sodium
   beef broth

1 tablespoon salt

1½ teaspoons freshly ground black pepper

½ teaspoon crushed red pepper

1 teaspoon dried oregano

1 teaspoon dried basil

1 teaspoon dried thyme

1½ teaspoons sugar

Lasagna

One 15-ounce container ricotta cheese

1 egg, beaten

1 package dried lasagna noodles (9 noodles),
   ends broken and discarded so the noodles
   are the length of the slow cooker

12 ounces packaged mozzarella cheese, grated

8 ounces sliced provolone cheese

8 ounces fresh mozzarella cheese,
   sliced

⅓ cup finely grated Parmigiano-Reggiano
   cheese

1. To make the meat sauce, heat a 12- to 14-inch skillet over medium-high heat. Add the beef, veal, and pork and cook, stirring as needed, until browned, about 8 minutes. Add the celery, onion, and garlic and cook for 2 minutes longer. Stir in the tomatoes, beef stock, salt, black pepper, crushed red pepper, oregano, basil, thyme, and sugar and simmer for 5 minutes. Remove from the heat and set aside to cool. (This sauce can be made up to several days in advance. It freezes well, too.)

2. Combine the ricotta and the egg in a medium bowl. Stir in ½ cup of the cooled meat sauce.

3. To assemble the lasagna, add ½ cup of the sauce to a 6-quart slow cooker. Arrange 3 lasagna noodles, side by side, on top of the sauce. Place 6 heaping tablespoons of the ricotta mixture on the noodles and spread it

out evenly. Top the noodles with one-third of the grated mozzarella, one-third of the provolone slices, and one-third of the fresh mozzarella. Top with 2 cups of the meat sauce. Make two more layers *without* adding the last layer of cheeses.

4. Cook on low for 4 hours.

5. Add the reserved cheeses and the Parmesan to the lasagna and replace the lid. Turn off the slow cooker and allow the cheese to melt and the lasagna to set up by letting it cool for at least 30 minutes before serving.

Pot Roast Dianne

We are turning steak with cognac and shallot sauce on its head and serving it up in the slow cooker. This is delicious, and just when you thought you couldn't find another way to enjoy a great roast!

1½ pounds small to medium Red Bliss potatoes, quartered

1 pound carrots, cut into 3-inch lengths

1 pound shallots, peeled, halved if large, with root end left intact

3 teaspoons salt

1½ teaspoons freshly ground black pepper, plus more for garnish

One 3½- to 4-pound bone-in beef chuck roast

8 cloves garlic, sliced

1 cup homemade beef stock (see page 6) or packaged low-sodium beef broth

6 tablespoons cognac

4 teaspoons Worcestershire sauce

2 teaspoons Dijon mustard

2 teaspoons freshly squeezed lemon juice

4 tablespoons (½ stick) unsalted butter, at room temperature

¼ cup all-purpose flour

½ cup chopped fresh parsley leaves, plus more for garnish

Fleur de sel, for garnish, if desired

Hot crusty bread, for serving

1. Add the potatoes, carrots, shallots, 1 teaspoon of the salt, and ¾ teaspoon of the pepper to a 6-quart slow cooker.

2. Using the tip of a paring knife, make deep narrow slits all over the roast, and insert 1 piece of garlic deep into each slit. Season the roast all over with the remaining 2 teaspoons salt and ¾ teaspoon pepper. Transfer the roast to the slow cooker and nestle it among the vegetables if space allows. Otherwise, let it rest on top.

3. In a small container, whisk together the beef stock, cognac, Worcestershire sauce, mustard, and lemon juice. Pour this into the slow cooker.

4. Cook on high for 7 hours, until the meat is tender.

5. Combine the butter and flour in a small bowl, and mash with the back of a spoon or a small spatula until uniform to make a beurre manié. During the last 10 minutes of cooking, transfer the roast and vegetables from the slow cooker to a platter and set aside. In three parts, whisk the beurre manié into the jus left in the cooker until incorporated. Stir in the ½ cup chopped parsley. Carve the roast into the desired portions, or slice it thinly, and return the meat and the vegetables to the slow cooker.

6. Serve the pot roast, vegetables, and hot sauce topped with additional chopped parsley, fleur de sel if desired, and freshly ground black pepper. Don't forget the crusty bread for mopping up the delicious sauce!

Slow-Cooked Barbecued Baby Back Ribs

This is seriously the simplest recipe for ribs. The meat is literally falling off the bone! The sauce is a snap to put together, but beware: it does have a little kick. The recipe makes more sauce than you need; store the extra in an airtight container in the refrigerator for at least 8 weeks and use it as you would any other barbecue sauce.

3 tablespoons unsalted butter
1 large yellow onion, finely chopped
2 cloves garlic, minced
½ cup cider vinegar
½ cup packed dark brown sugar
¼ cup molasses
2 tablespoons honey
2 tablespoons Worcestershire sauce
2 tablespoons dark rum
2 tablespoons dry mustard
1 tablespoon pimentón picante
    (hot smoked Spanish paprika)
2 teaspoons crushed red pepper
2 teaspoons kosher salt,
    plus more to season the ribs
1 teaspoon freshly ground black pepper,
    plus more to season the ribs
½ teaspoon ground allspice

2 cups ketchup
One 12-ounce bottle Heinz chili sauce
3 racks baby back ribs (about 6 pounds total)

1. In a heavy-bottomed 1½-quart saucepan, melt the butter over medium heat. Add the onion and garlic and cook for 5 minutes, or until the onion is soft and translucent. Add all the remaining ingredients except the ribs, and cook over medium heat, stirring as needed, until the flavors come together and sauce has thickened to the desired consistency, about 30 minutes. The sauce may be used immediately or transferred to jars, cooled to room temperature, covered, and refrigerated. The sauce will keep for up to 2 months.

2. Cut each rack of ribs into 2 portions and season both sides of the ribs with salt and pepper. Brush the ribs liberally with some of the sauce and place them in a 6-quart slow cooker, shingled one on top of the other.

3. Cook on high for 7 hours.

4. Cut into individual ribs to serve, if desired, and pass additional sauce for dipping.

Gingered Short Ribs and Carrots

You already know how succulent short ribs are when cooked in a slow cooker: low and slow is the perfect way to bring out every bit of tenderness and flavor. The ginger and Chinese five-spice powder here add a spicy twist. The ribs are coated with the spices and then refrigerated overnight for the best flavor, so keep this in mind when planning your cook time.

2 tablespoons sugar

2½ teaspoons Chinese five-spice powder

1 tablespoon plus 1 teaspoon kosher salt

¾ teaspoon freshly ground black pepper

½ teaspoon Chinese or Colman's dry mustard

4 pounds beef short ribs

1 pound carrots, cut into 3-inch lengths

1 large yellow onion, cut into large chunks

1 medium green bell pepper, cored, seeded, and cut into 1-inch-wide strips

1 medium red bell pepper, cored, seeded, and cut into 1-inch-wide strips

4 tablespoons chopped fresh ginger

4 tablespoons chopped garlic (8 to 10 large cloves)

4 tablespoons soy sauce

1 teaspoon crushed red pepper, or 2 whole dried red chiles

1 cup homemade beef stock (see page 6) or packaged low-sodium beef broth

¼ cup cornstarch

2 bunches green onions, cut into 3-inch lengths, for garnish

Hot steamed jasmine rice, for serving

1. Combine the sugar, five-spice powder, the 1 tablespoon salt, the black pepper, and mustard in a large bowl. Add the ribs and toss well until evenly coated with the spice mixture. Cover with plastic wrap and refrigerate overnight.

2. Preheat the oven to 450°F.

3. Season the short ribs with the remaining teaspoon of salt and lay them on a rack set in a roasting pan. Roast in the oven for 20 to 25 minutes, until some of the fat is rendered and the ribs are browned.

4. Meanwhile, add the carrots, onion, bell peppers, ginger, garlic, soy sauce, and crushed red pepper to a 6-quart slow cooker. Pour in the beef stock. When the ribs are browned, add them to the slow cooker.

5. Cook on high for 6 hours or on low for 8 hours, until the meat is fork-tender.

6. During the last 10 minutes of cooking, remove the ribs from the slow cooker and set them aside. Put the cornstarch in a small bowl, and stir in ¼ cup of the liquid from the slow cooker, blending it in thoroughly. Whisk this mixture into the slow cooker to thicken the broth. Return the ribs to the slow cooker so that they stay warm until you are ready to serve.

7. Right before serving, remove the whole chiles if using, and add the green onions to the slow cooker. Serve the short ribs and vegetables over hot steamed rice in individual bowls.

White Chocolate Pots de Crème

Pot de crème is a French dessert, literally translated as "pot of cream." Pots de crème are small custards that are not usually as firm as a flan or a crème caramel, and for this reason they are cooked in individual pot de crème pots or ramekins. I suggest using a high-quality white chocolate for this recipe for the best results. If you happen not to like white chocolate, you can easily substitute semisweet or bittersweet chocolate.

1¼ cups heavy cream
3½ ounces white chocolate,
    chopped
1 vanilla bean, pod split open,
    seeds scraped out and reserved
⅓ cup sugar
3 large egg yolks
1½ cups hot water, or more if
    needed

1. Heat the cream in a small saucepan over medium heat just until it begins to simmer. Remove the pan from the heat and add the chocolate, the vanilla pod (cut in half to fit if necessary), and the vanilla seeds. Let steep for at least 10 minutes.

2. Remove the vanilla bean (set it aside for another use or discard it), and whisk the cream mixture to blend it well.

3. In a small heat-proof mixing bowl, whisk the sugar and egg yolks together until the yolks are pale yellow and frothy.

4. Slowly whisk the cream mixture into the egg yolks. Whisk continuously until combined. Strain the mixture through a fine-mesh sieve into another bowl. Divide the mixture equally among six ½-cup ramekins.

5. Place a kitchen towel or a rack in the bottom of a 6-quart slow cooker, and add the hot water. Gently place the ramekins in the slow cooker. If necessary, add more hot water so that it reaches halfway up the sides of the ramekins.

6. Cook on high for 1½ hours.

7. Carefully remove the pots de crème from the slow cooker and transfer them to a baking sheet. Place them in the refrigerator to cool. Once cooled, the pots de crème can be covered with plastic wrap and stored in the refrigerator for up to 24 hours.

8. Allow the pots de crème to come almost to room temperature before serving.

The Multi-Cooker:
A lean, mean all-purpose machine

A Note on Multi-Cookers

All the recipes in this chapter were tested in the Emeril by T-fal Rice and Multi-Cooker. Although it's unique in that it functions as a rice cooker as well as a multi-cooker, you can also prepare these recipes in an electric multi-cooker with variable cooking programs or in a rice cooker that has cooking programs other than rice (such as steam, grains, simmer, sauté). Because of various products' differences in cooking programs and temperature settings, cook times may have to be adjusted. Get to know your multi-cooker!

I've listed the programs that the Emeril Rice and Multi-Cooker features below, along with a general guide to what can be cooked using the various programs. This should help you adapt the recipes that follow to your multi-cooker or rice cooker by comparing settings. Note that you will need a rice or multi-cooker that has a bowl with at least a 4-quart capacity and in which you can sauté directly in the bowl. In our multi-cooker we are able to sauté on either the "white rice" setting or the "steam" setting; other multi-cookers have programs exclusively for sautéing, and I would suggest trying that program when we advise to sauté in the recipes here.

➢ WHITE RICE: used to cook all types of white rice, including sticky rice and Arborio rice. Also perfect for sautéing ingredients with the lid open.

➢ QUICK RICE: used for quick-cooking (parcooked) rice.

➢ BROWN RICE: used for cooking brown rice and wild rice.

➢ WHOLE GRAINS: great for cooking whole grains and polenta.

➢ OATMEAL: for making perfect oatmeal.

The Multi-Cooker

➤ SLOW COOK: functions like a typical slow cooker.

➤ STEAM: perfect for steaming vegetables, fish, or chicken. Ours also has a steamer basket that enables you to cook in both the bowl and the basket at the same time if desired. This setting is also suitable for light sautéing.

➤ DESSERT: perfect for cooking sponge cakes.

If you're in the market for a multi-cooker, here are a few recommended features:

➤ As many variable cooking programs as possible, such as "steam," "sauté" or "brown," "simmer," "slow cook," and so on.

➤ Ability to sauté right in the bowl.

➤ A "keep warm" setting so that food stays hot after cooking is complete.

➤ A built-in timer.

➤ Bowl capacity of at least 4 quarts.

➤ A steamer basket insert.

Beluga Lentil Salad

Cream of Cauliflower Soup

This is the ultimate comfort food! Once blended, the soup has a silky-smooth texture and is subtly flavored with just a hint of saffron. Enjoy it in a mug while sitting next to a warm fire, or serve it to your dinner guests as a light appetizer—either way, it is sure to please.

2 tablespoons unsalted butter

1 cup thinly sliced yellow onion (about 1 medium onion)

2 cloves garlic, thinly sliced

1 medium head cauliflower, cut into florets

6 cups homemade chicken stock (see page 5) or packaged low-sodium chicken broth, plus more if needed

2 cups half-and-half, plus more if needed

1 tablespoon kosher salt

½ teaspoon cayenne pepper

¼ teaspoon saffron threads, plus more for garnish

½ cup sliced almonds, toasted (see below), for garnish

Extra-virgin olive oil, for garnish

1. Set a multi-cooker on the "white rice" program and add the butter. When the butter begins to bubble, add the onion and garlic. Cook until they are soft, about 10 minutes. Add the cauliflower, chicken stock, half-and-half, salt, cayenne pepper, and saffron to the multi-cooker.

2. Close the lid, set the multi-cooker to the "steam" program, and cook for 35 minutes.

3. Transfer the soup to a blender and puree until smooth (see Note). If the soup is too thick, add more chicken stock or half-and-half to thin it to the desired consistency.

4. Garnish the soup with the toasted almonds, a drizzle of olive oil, and a few threads of saffron.

NOTE: *Use caution when blending hot liquids: blend only small amounts at a time, with the blender tightly covered and a kitchen towel held over the top.*

Toasting Nuts

Nuts of choice, up to 3 cups per baking sheet

1. Position an oven rack in the center and preheat the oven to 350°F.

2. Spread the nuts on baking sheets. Bake until golden and fragrant, 8 to 10 minutes.

3. Transfer the baking sheets to a wire rack to cool.

4. Use as desired or store in an airtight container in a cool, dry location for up to 2 weeks.

NOTE: *Whole nuts or halves are best for toasting and can be chopped easily once they have cooled.*

Potato Soup with Bacon and Cheddar

You could almost call this "baked potato soup," but I didn't, since in that case you'd have to use your oven. Here you get all the flavors simmered away in your multi-cooker in just under an hour. This soup is hearty enough on its own, but you could easily stir in baby spinach at the end to boost it with another vegetable, or serve it alongside a salad and roast chicken. Or hey, even a steak.

4 strips bacon, diced
2 cups chopped yellow onion
    (about 2 medium onions)
¼ cup minced shallot
    (about 1 medium shallot)
1 tablespoon minced garlic
    (about 4 large cloves)
1½ pounds Idaho potatoes,
    peeled and cut into ½-inch chunks,
    submerged in a bowl of water
1 pound Yukon Gold potatoes,
    peeled and cut into ½-inch chunks,
    submerged in a bowl of water
1 pound small Red Bliss potatoes,
    skin on, halved or quartered,
    submerged in a bowl of water
6 cups homemade chicken stock
    (see page 5) or packaged
    low-sodium chicken broth
1 teaspoon salt
¼ teaspoon freshly ground white pepper

¼ teaspoon freshly ground black pepper,
    plus more for garnish
½ cup heavy cream
2 tablespoons chopped fresh chives,
    plus more for garnish
8 ounces sharp cheddar cheese,
    grated, for garnish

1. Set a multi-cooker to the "steam" program, add the bacon, and cook for 5 minutes, or until it begins to brown. Stir in the onion, shallot, and garlic and cook for 5 minutes longer. Drain the potatoes and add them to the multi-cooker along with the chicken stock, salt, white pepper, and black pepper.

2. Close the lid and cook for about 50 minutes, until the potatoes are tender.

3. Set the multi-cooker to "warm" and stir in the heavy cream and chives. Serve the soup in bowls, garnished with the cheddar and sprinkled with additional chives and black pepper as desired.

Shrimp Bisque

You can easily make crème fraîche yourself: Pour 1 cup of heavy cream into a jar, stir in 2 tablespoons of buttermilk, and set it aside, covered, for 8 to 12 hours. Stir it again, cover, and refrigerate overnight. You will have a wonderfully soured thickened cream that can last up to a week in your fridge. If you don't have time to make your own and can't find it in the store, just stir ¼ cup of heavy cream into the soup right before serving.

4 tablespoons (½ stick) unsalted butter

1 cup chopped yellow onion (about 1 medium onion)

½ cup chopped celery (about 1 rib celery)

½ cup chopped carrot (about 1 medium carrot)

3 cloves garlic, smashed

2 tablespoons tomato paste

¾ cup brandy

2 cups bottled clam juice

1 sprig fresh thyme, plus 2 teaspoons fresh thyme leaves

¼ teaspoon cayenne pepper

2 teaspoons salt, plus more for seasoning

1½ pounds shrimp, peeled and deveined

5 cups water

½ cup long-grain white rice

Freshly ground black pepper

½ cup crème fraîche, for serving

1. Set a multi-cooker to the "steam" program. Add 3 tablespoons of the butter and when it has melted, add the onion, celery, carrot, and garlic and cook for 5 minutes. Stir in the tomato paste and brandy and cook for 2 minutes longer. Add the clam juice, thyme sprig, cayenne, salt, 1 pound of the shrimp, and the water.

2. Close the lid and cook for 25 minutes. Stir in the rice, close the lid, and cook for another 25 minutes. Turn off the multi-cooker and allow the soup to cool slightly. Discard the sprig of thyme.

3. While the soup is cooling, chop the remaining ½ pound of shrimp into large pieces. Set a small sauté pan over medium-high heat and add the remaining 1 tablespoon butter. When the butter has melted, add the shrimp and sauté until just cooked through, about 1 minute. Remove from the heat, stir in the fresh thyme leaves, and season with salt and black pepper. Cover and keep warm.

4. In batches, puree the soup in a blender for 2 minutes (see Note), transferring each batch to a large pot or container. Return the pureed soup to the multi-cooker and set it to "warm." Serve the bisque hot, garnished with the sautéed shrimp and a dollop of crème fraîche.

NOTE: *Use caution when blending hot liquids: blend only small amounts at a time, with the blender tightly covered and a kitchen towel held over the top.*

Seafood Soup with Coconut Milk and Tamarind

The ease of making this soup and the intensity of its flavor are both unbelievable. Tart, spicy, and creamy all at once, this Thai-inspired soup is not to be missed.

1 tablespoon vegetable oil

1½ cups sliced red bell pepper
   (about 1 medium pepper)

1½ cups sliced yellow onion
   (about 1 large onion)

2 tablespoons minced fresh ginger

2 tablespoons minced fresh garlic
   (4 to 5 large cloves)

4 cups small cauliflower florets
   (from about 8 ounces)

6 cups homemade chicken stock (see page 5)
   or packaged low-sodium chicken broth

One 13- or 14.5-ounce can unsweetened
   coconut milk

¼ cup Thai fish sauce

2 tablespoons light brown sugar

1 tablespoon chili garlic sauce,
   plus more for garnish

2 teaspoons tamarind concentrate, or 2
   tablespoons freshly squeezed lime juice

1 pound mussels, cleaned

1 pound cod fillet, cut into ½-inch chunks

1 pound peeled and deveined shrimp,
   halved lengthwise

½ cup chopped fresh cilantro leaves

½ cup chopped fresh basil leaves

1. Set a multi-cooker to the "steam" program, add the oil, and heat for 5 minutes. Add the bell pepper and onion and cook, stirring as needed, for 10 minutes. Stir in the ginger, garlic, and cauliflower and cook for 2 minutes longer. Add the chicken stock, coconut milk, fish sauce, brown sugar, chili garlic sauce, and tamarind concentrate.

2. Close the lid and cook the soup for 35 minutes. Add the mussels, close the lid, and cook for 10 minutes more. Add the cod and shrimp, close the lid, and cook for 5 minutes longer, or until all the mussels have opened and all the seafood is cooked through. Stir in the cilantro and basil. Serve immediately, with additional chili garlic sauce as desired.

Wilted Escarole with Garlic and Crushed Red Pepper

The Italians know a thing or two about preparing vegetables, and one of my favorites that they do so well is escarole. Many Americans shy away from escarole because of its slightly bitter flavor, but when paired with nutty garlic, spicy crushed red pepper, and a hint of salt and lemon, it's transported to another level. This is based on the classic Italian preparation, just made nearly foolproof in the multi-cooker.

¼ cup extra-virgin olive oil,
    plus more for drizzling
12 cloves garlic, thinly sliced
½ teaspoon crushed red pepper
1¼ cups homemade chicken stock
    (see page 5) or packaged low-sodium
    chicken broth
2 large heads (about 2 pounds) escarole,
    cleaned, cut into 1-inch-wide strips
1½ teaspoons kosher salt,
    plus more for garnish
¼ teaspoon freshly ground black pepper
Freshly squeezed lemon juice, to taste
Finely grated Parmigiano-Reggiano cheese,
    for garnish (optional)

1. In a multi-cooker set to the "steam" program, heat the olive oil. When it is hot, add the garlic and crushed red pepper and cook until the garlic is lightly golden around the edges and fragrant, 2 to 3 minutes. Add the chicken stock, bring to a boil, and cook for 2 minutes.

2. Add the escarole, in batches, stirring frequently and adding more as the previous addition wilts. Season with the salt and black pepper and cook until the greens are slightly wilted but still crisp-tender, 7 to 10 minutes.

3. Serve the escarole immediately, drizzled with olive oil and lemon juice, and sprinkled with salt and, if desired, grated Parmesan.

Baby Bok Choy with Black Bean–Garlic Sauce

If you've never thought of cooking bok choy in your multi-cooker, think again! The "steam" program functions beautifully to cook this tender veggie just right. The sauce is simply stirred together and then cooked just long enough to thicken. Serve this as a side dish, or as a main course by offering it with steamed jasmine rice.

⅓ cup homemade chicken stock (see page 5) or packaged low-sodium chicken broth

2 tablespoons Chinese rice wine

½ teaspoon dark Asian sesame oil

2 teaspoons cornstarch

2 teaspoons black bean sauce (see Note)

1 teaspoon chili garlic sauce

1 teaspoon soy sauce

¼ teaspoon crushed red pepper

3 tablespoons vegetable oil

2 pounds baby bok choy, halved or quartered lengthwise

2 tablespoons minced garlic (4 to 5 large cloves)

1. In a small bowl, stir together the chicken stock, rice wine, sesame oil, cornstarch, black bean sauce, chili garlic sauce, soy sauce, and crushed red pepper. Set aside.

2. Set a multi-cooker to the "steam" program and add 1 tablespoon of the vegetable oil. When the oil is hot but not quite smoking, add one-third of the bok choy and one-third of the garlic. Cook, stirring, until crisp-tender, 3 to 5 minutes (this will depend on the size of bok choy and may take longer for mature bok choy). Transfer the bok choy to a serving dish and repeat two more times with the remaining oil, bok choy, and garlic. When all of the bok choy has been cooked, stir the sauce mixture and add it to the multi-cooker. Cook, stirring constantly, until the sauce has thickened, about 2 minutes. Drizzle the hot sauce over the bok choy and serve immediately.

NOTE: *Black bean sauce can be found in Asian specialty markets and sometimes in the international section of your grocery store. It's made from fermented black beans and has a pungent, salty flavor.*

Brussels Sprouts Amandine

You will love these. Brussels sprouts are tossed in lemon, butter, parsley, and toasted almonds for a twist on the classic dish. Go ahead and sauté your favorite fish and put *it* on the side.

2 cups water

2 pounds Brussels sprouts,
    cut in half or quartered if large

¾ teaspoon salt

½ teaspoon freshly ground black pepper

6 tablespoons (¾ stick) unsalted butter

½ cup chopped shallots
    (about 2 medium shallots)

1 teaspoon minced garlic
    (about 1 large clove)

1 cup sliced almonds

2 tablespoons freshly squeezed lemon juice

2 tablespoons chopped fresh parsley leaves

1. Add the water to a multi-cooker and insert the steamer basket. Add the Brussels sprouts to the steamer basket. Season them with ¼ teaspoon of the salt and ¼ teaspoon of the pepper. Close the lid and set the multi-cooker to the "steam" program. Cook the Brussels sprouts until crisp-tender, 20 to 22 minutes, or to the desired texture. Transfer the Brussels sprouts to a bowl and set aside. Discard the water in the multi-cooker.

2. Continuing to cook on the "steam" program, add the butter to the multi-cooker. Once the butter has melted, stir in the shallot and garlic, and sauté for 3 minutes, or until the shallot has softened. Stir in the almonds. Toast the almonds in the butter, stirring frequently, until lightly browned, about 10 minutes. Add the lemon juice, parsley, and the remaining ½ teaspoon salt and ¼ teaspoon pepper. Return the Brussels sprouts to the multi-cooker and stir to coat with the shallot, almonds, and butter. Set the multi-cooker to "warm" and serve immediately.

Emeril's Kicked-Up Creamed Spinach

Here's the ultimate, most decadent version of this recipe yet! I've added triple-cream Brie to this spinach to really kick it up a notch. It's so good you'll go back for seconds and thirds.

4 tablespoons (½ stick) unsalted butter,
    plus 2 tablespoons at room temperature
1 medium yellow onion, chopped
1 tablespoon minced garlic
    (2 to 3 cloves)
1¼ teaspoons sea salt
2 pounds prewashed baby spinach
8 ounces Neufchâtel cheese,
    cubed
8 ounces triple-cream Brie cheese,
    cut into ¼-inch cubes
½ cup grated Parmigiano-Reggiano cheese
½ teaspoon freshly ground black pepper
¼ teaspoon crushed red pepper
2 tablespoons all-purpose flour

1. Set the multi-cooker to the "white rice" program and add the 4 tablespoons butter. When the butter begins to bubble, add the onion, garlic, and ½ teaspoon of the salt. Cook the onion and garlic until translucent, 10 to 12 minutes. Add the spinach in batches, stirring after each addition and cooking until all the spinach has wilted, 7 to 9 minutes. Stir in the Neufchâtel, Brie, Parmesan, the remaining salt, the black pepper, and crushed red pepper. Close the lid and cook for 20 minutes.

2. In a small bowl, make a beurre manié by mixing the 2 tablespoons room-temperature butter and the flour with a fork until you have formed a smooth paste. Stir the beurre manié into the spinach mixture and cook, stirring, for 10 minutes, or until the mixture thickens.

3. Serve immediately, or let cool and store in an airtight container in the refrigerator for up to 3 days. If refrigerated, reheat gently in the microwave before serving.

Basmati Rice with Caramelized Onions

Fragrant basmati rice combines with caramelized onions, fresh vegetables, and aromatic spices in a dish inspired by the biryanis and pilaus of India. Serve this with a yogurt raita and your favorite chutney, or alongside stewed chickpeas, split peas, or roast meats.

5 tablespoons ghee (see Notes)
    or clarified butter
4 large yellow onions,
    halved and thinly sliced crosswise
2½ teaspoons kosher salt
2 cups basmati rice
8 cardamom pods, smashed with the side
    of a knife (see Notes)
6 whole cloves (see Notes)
One 3-inch piece cinnamon stick,
    broken in half
1 teaspoon cumin seeds
1 teaspoon garam masala
¾ teaspoon ground turmeric
2½ cups homemade chicken stock
    (see page 5) or packaged low-sodium
    chicken or vegetable broth
3 cups diced mixed vegetables,
    such as carrots, parsnips,
    okra, and green beans (½-inch dice)
2 cups cauliflower or broccoli florets
½ cup chopped toasted unsalted pistachios
    (see page 66)

½ cup chopped toasted walnuts
    (see page 66)
¼ cup dried currants
¼ cup golden raisins
¼ cup chopped fresh cilantro leaves

1. In the bowl of a multi-cooker set on the "white rice" program, melt 4 tablespoons of the ghee. Add the onions and ½ teaspoon of the salt and cook, uncovered and stirring occasionally, until the onions are caramelized, 45 minutes to 1 hour. You will need to stir the onions more frequently near the end of the cooking so that they do not scorch.

2. While the onions are cooking, place the rice in a fine-mesh sieve and rinse it several times under cool running water, until the water that runs off the rice is mostly clear. Transfer the rice to a bowl and add enough cool water to cover. Set aside to soak for 30 minutes, then drain.

3. Once the onions are caramelized, remove roughly two-thirds of them from the multi-cooker and set them aside. Add the remaining 1 tablespoon ghee to the multi-cooker along with the drained rice, the remaining 2 teaspoons salt, and the cardamom pods, cloves, cinnamon sticks, cumin, garam masala, and turmeric. Cook, stirring, until the rice is fragrant, 2 to 3

minutes. Add the chicken stock and the diced vegetables, and close the lid. Reset the multi-cooker to the "white rice" program and cook for 15 minutes.

4. Open the lid and gently toss the rice and vegetables, stirring to get the rice from the bottom of the pot fully integrated with the remaining grains. Add the cauliflower on top of the rice, close the lid, and cook for 10 minutes more.

5. Turn the multi-cooker off and allow it to sit undisturbed for 5 minutes. Then fluff the rice with a fork and turn it out onto a serving bowl or platter. Remove and discard the cinnamon sticks. Top the rice evenly with the reserved caramelized onions and the pistachios, walnuts, currants, golden raisins, and cilantro. Serve hot or warm.

NOTES: *Ghee is butter that has been melted slowly until the solids and liquid separate. The solids fall to the bottom, and the butter is cooked until the milk solids are browned and the moisture evaporates, resulting in a nutty, caramel-like flavor. This last step is what distinguishes ghee from regular clarified butter. In both ghee and clarified butter, the milk solids are strained out and discarded before using. Ghee is used primarily in Indian cooking but is wonderful for any high-heat cooking preparation because it has a higher smoke point than butter. You can find it in many Middle Eastern markets, or you can easily make your own at home.*

I like getting a surprising taste of cardamom or clove every now and again when eating this rice, but if you don't like running into these inedible spices, simply tie them up in a small piece of cheesecloth before cooking and then remove them before serving.

Goat Cheese and Orzo–Stuffed Tomatoes

Some of the simplest things can be some of the best. Take beautiful firm-ripe tomatoes, prepare a simple sausage and orzo stuffing, and steam them until tender, and you have a picture-perfect side dish or entrée. This dish is best when tomatoes are at their ripest and most flavorful. But you could also use this filling to stuff zucchini, squash, or peppers if ripe tomatoes are not readily available.

8 medium heirloom tomatoes
4 tablespoons extra-virgin olive oil
8 ounces fresh mild Italian sausage,
    preferably in bulk
1 small yellow onion, finely diced
1 tablespoon minced garlic
    (2 to 3 large cloves)
1 large zucchini, grated
1 teaspoon kosher salt
½ teaspoon freshly ground black pepper
1 cup cooked orzo pasta
    (from about ¾ cup dry orzo)
4 ounces aged goat cheese,
    crumbled
2 tablespoons chopped fresh basil leaves
1 tablespoon chopped fresh mint leaves
½ cup finely grated Parmigiano-Reggiano
    cheese
½ cup panko breadcrumbs, toasted
    (see Note)

1. Using a sharp paring knife, remove the top (stem end) of the tomatoes and set the tops aside. Scoop out the meat and pulp from the inside of the tomatoes, leaving the tomato shells intact, and place the pulp in a fine-mesh sieve set over a small bowl. Using the back of a spoon or your hands, press the pulp through the sieve. Discard the seeds and any remaining tough pulp in the sieve; reserve the tomato juice.

2. Heat a large sauté pan over medium heat. When it is hot, add 2 tablespoons of the olive oil and the sausage, and brown the sausage, breaking it up as you cook, about 2 minutes. Using a slotted spoon, transfer the sausage to a paper-towel-lined plate.

3. Add the onion, garlic, and zucchini to the sauté pan, season with ½ teaspoon of the salt and ¼ teaspoon of the pepper, and sauté until the onion is tender, 4 to 5 minutes.

4. In a medium mixing bowl, combine the sausage, onion mixture, and cooked orzo, and mix well. Gently fold in the goat cheese, basil, and mint.

5. In a small bowl, combine the Parmesan and panko.

6. Season the inside of the tomatoes with the remaining ½ teaspoon salt and ¼

teaspoon pepper. Divide the Parmesan-panko mixture among the tomatoes.

7. Using a spoon, fill the tomatoes with the orzo-sausage stuffing. Place the tomatoes in the steamer basket of a multi-cooker and replace the tomato tops. Depending on the size of your tomatoes, you may need to cook them in two batches.

8. Pour the reserved tomato juice into the bowl of the multi-cooker, add the steamer insert with the tomatoes, close the lid, and set the machine to the "steam" program. Cook for 15 to 18 minutes, or until the tomatoes are tender but still firm enough to hold their stuffing.

9. Serve the stuffed tomatoes immediately, drizzled with any remaining tomato juice from the bowl of the multi-cooker and the remaining olive oil.

NOTE: *Panko breadcrumbs can be toasted in a dry nonstick skillet over medium heat. Cook, stirring frequently with a heatproof rubber spatula to promote even browning, until golden, about 5 minutes.*

Barley Risotto with Spring Vegetables

Barley is at the top of my list because it's both hearty and healthy. During the cooking process here, the barley naturally becomes creamy while maintaining a slightly chewy texture. This dish highlights spring vegetables, so feel free to use whatever may be available in your neck of the woods.

5 cups homemade chicken stock (see page 5) or packaged low-sodium chicken broth

2 tablespoons olive oil

1 medium yellow onion, diced

1 clove garlic, minced

1 teaspoon chopped fresh thyme leaves, plus more for garnish

1 bay leaf

2 cups pearl barley

½ cup dry white wine

1½ teaspoons kosher salt

½ teaspoon freshly ground white pepper

1 pound asparagus, ends trimmed, spears cut on the diagonal into 1-inch lengths

1 cup baby radishes, cut in half or quarters

1 cup sweet spring peas

½ cup mascarpone cheese or crème fraîche

4 ounces thinly sliced prosciutto

½ cup freshly grated Parmigiano-Reggiano cheese

Chiffonade of fresh basil leaves, for garnish

1. In a small saucepan, bring the chicken stock to a boil over medium-high heat and then reduce it to a low simmer. Keep the heat on low.

2. Set a multi-cooker to the "white rice" program, and when it is hot, add the oil, onion, and garlic. Sauté until the onion and garlic are soft and translucent, about 10 minutes. Add the thyme, bay leaf, barley, and white wine. Season with 1 teaspoon of the salt and ¼ teaspoon of the white pepper, and cook until the wine has evaporated, about 4 minutes. Add the hot stock, close the lid, reset to the "white rice" program, and cook for 30 minutes.

3. Open the multi-cooker and stir the barley. Place the asparagus and radishes in the steamer basket, and season with the remaining ½ teaspoon salt and ¼ teaspoon white pepper. Place the steamer basket in the multi-cooker, close the lid, and cook for 15 minutes.

4. Carefully remove the steamer basket and add the asparagus, radishes, peas, and mascarpone to the barley. Stir gently, close the lid, and cook for 15 minutes.

5. In a small sauté pan set over medium-high heat, crisp the prosciutto in batches. Transfer it from the pan to a paper-towel-lined plate.

6. Just before serving the barley, remove the bay leaf, sprinkle the barley with the grated Parmesan, crumble the prosciutto on top, and add the basil chiffonade.

Black-Eyed Peas and Rice

This is the treasured rice dish known as Hoppin' John, and it's easy to make in your multi-cooker. The machine performs double duty: first it slow-cooks your beans, then it steams your rice. Traditionally served on New Year's Day for good luck, this is delicious anytime.

1 pound dried black-eyed peas

6½ cups homemade chicken stock
    (see page 5) or packaged low-sodium
    chicken broth

12 ounces smoked ham hock

1 cup chopped yellow onion
    (about 1 medium onion)

½ cup chopped celery (about 1 rib)

½ cup chopped green bell pepper
    (about ½ medium pepper)

1 tablespoon minced garlic
    (2 to 3 cloves)

½ teaspoon crushed red pepper

1 large bay leaf

1½ teaspoons salt

½ teaspoon freshly ground black pepper

1 cup long-grain white rice, rinsed

Hot sauce, for serving

1. Add all the ingredients except the rice and hot sauce to a multi-cooker, close the lid, and set the machine to the "slow cook" program for 2 hours.

2. When the beans have finished cooking, stir in the rice, close the lid, and set the multi-cooker to the "white rice" program.

3. Once the cooking is complete, remove and discard the bay leaf and transfer the ham hock to a plate. When it is cool enough to handle, discard the rind, fat, and bone. Shred the meat.

4. Gently fluff the rice and peas with a fork and serve hot, garnished with some of the ham hock meat. Pass the hot sauce for guests to use to their liking.

Beluga Lentil Salad

Beluga lentils, the smallest of the lentil family, look like glistening black caviar once they're cooked. This particular lentil cooks quickly and really holds its shape. The salad makes a great accompaniment to grilled fish or poultry but is completely satisfying all on its own.

2 cups beluga lentils

2 yellow onions, quartered

2 carrots, cut into 3-inch lengths

2 ribs celery, cut into 3-inch lengths

2 bay leaves

4 cups water

2 teaspoons kosher salt,
    plus more for the dressing

1 teaspoon freshly ground black pepper,
    plus more for the dressing

2 tablespoons minced shallot

1 tablespoon Dijon mustard

2 teaspoons grated lemon zest

⅓ cup red wine vinegar

2 tablespoons freshly squeezed lemon juice

⅔ cup olive oil

3 tablespoons chopped
    fresh parsley leaves

3 tablespoons chopped
    fresh mint leaves

1 cup cherry tomatoes, halved

1 cup thinly sliced red onion
    (about 1 medium onion)

1 cup diced cucumber
    (about ¾ medium cucumber)

1 cup diced zucchini
    (about 1½ small zucchini)

1 cup crumbled feta cheese

Extra-virgin olive oil, for serving

Toasted peasant bread, for serving

1. Add the lentils, onions, carrots, celery, bay leaves, water, salt, and pepper to a multi-cooker. Set it to the "slow cook" program, close the lid, and cook for 4 hours. When the lentils are done, they will be tender but not mushy.

2. Drain the lentils in a colander, discarding the liquid. Discard the onions, carrots, celery, and bay leaves. Transfer the lentils to a medium bowl.

3. Prepare the vinaigrette by whisking the shallot, mustard, lemon zest, vinegar, and lemon juice in a small mixing bowl. While continuing to whisk, slowly drizzle in the olive oil until the mixture is emulsified. Whisk in the parsley and mint. Season to taste with salt and pepper. Pour the vinaigrette over the lentils and toss to combine.

4. In a large serving bowl, combine the cherry tomatoes, red onion, cucumber, and zucchini. Add the lentils and toss to combine. Sprinkle the feta cheese over the top.

5. Serve the lentils either warm or at room temperature, with a drizzle of olive oil on top and some toasted peasant bread alongside.

Stone-Ground Yellow Corn Grits

Since these grits are stone-ground, they'll have a thick, creamy texture. And as they sit and sit after cooking, they get better and better, becoming more and more tender. Though you still have to stir them from time to time in the multi-cooker, the ease of cooking can't be beat. Of course they're wonderful served with a pat of butter, but you can fancy them up with cheese, or serve them with a seared ham steak, sautéed shrimp, or grillades . . . delicious!

2 cups stone-ground yellow grits
1 tablespoon salt
1 teaspoon freshly ground black pepper
4 tablespoons (½ stick) unsalted butter
6 cups whole milk
6 cups water

1. Add the grits, salt, pepper, and 2 tablespoons of the butter to a multi-cooker. Stir in 4 cups of the milk and 4 cups of the water. Set the multi-cooker to the "whole grains" program, close the lid, and cook for 15 minutes.

2. Stir in the remaining 2 cups water, close the lid, and cook for 15 minutes.

3. Stir in the remaining 2 cups milk, close the lid, and cook for 15 minutes. Then stir the grits again, close the lid, and continue cooking for another 15 to 20 minutes, or until the grits are tender and creamy.

4. Stir in the remaining 2 tablespoons butter. Serve hot.

Creamy Polenta

Enjoy a bowl of this cheese-laced polenta as a decadent indulgence on its own, or serve it with your favorite stewed meat or poultry. It is great with either the Quick Osso Buco on page 170 or the Sunday Gravy on page 168.

8 cups water

2 cups yellow cornmeal

1½ tablespoons kosher salt

¼ teaspoon freshly ground white pepper

8 ounces mascarpone cheese or
    cream cheese, at room temperature

½ cup heavy cream

1 cup finely grated Parmigiano-Reggiano
    cheese, plus more for sprinkling

¼ cup extra-virgin olive oil,
    plus more for drizzling

1. In a large, heavy saucepan, bring the water to a boil over medium-high heat. While whisking constantly, slowly sprinkle the cornmeal into the water until completely combined. Continue to whisk, making sure there are no lumps. Add the salt and white pepper to the polenta, and then transfer it to a multi-cooker. Close the lid, set the multi-cooker to the "whole grains" program, and cook until the polenta is thickened and creamy, 35 to 40 minutes.

2. When the polenta is done, open the lid and whisk until smooth (it may be a little thicker around the edges). Add the mascarpone, heavy cream, Parmesan, and olive oil, and stir until smooth and creamy.

3. Serve the polenta hot, sprinkled with additional Parmesan cheese and drizzled with extra-virgin olive oil.

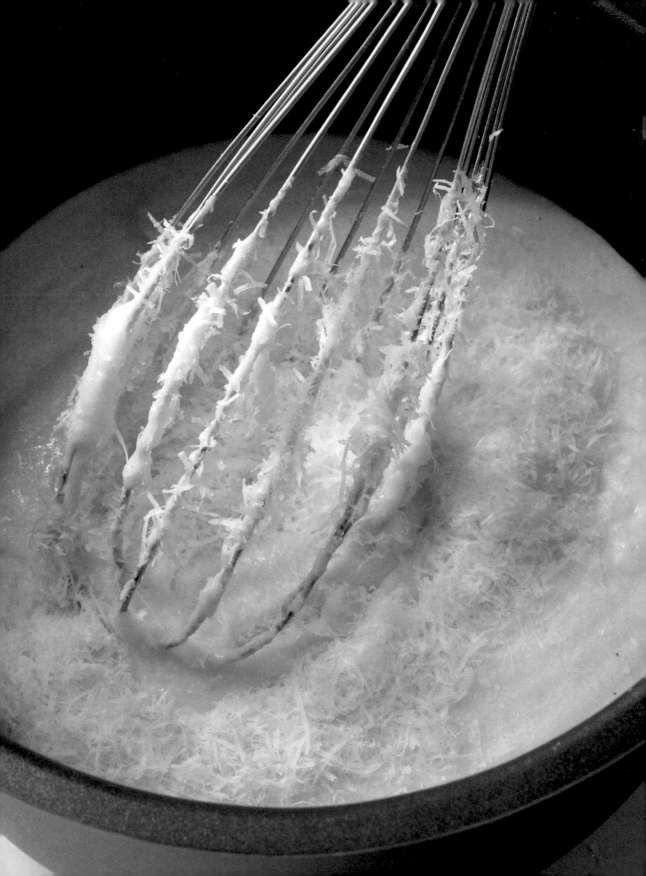

Cheese and Macaroni

The title of this recipe says it all. Sinfully delicious.

6 tablespoons (¾ stick) unsalted butter

½ cup chopped yellow onion
   (about ½ small onion)

1½ teaspoons minced garlic
   (about 2 large cloves)

1 teaspoon salt

¼ teaspoon freshly ground black pepper

Pinch of cayenne pepper

Pinch of sweet paprika

6 tablespoons all-purpose flour

5 cups whole milk

1 pound elbow macaroni, uncooked

8 ounces fresh mozzarella cheese, cut into
   pieces or sliced

4 ounces packaged whole-milk or part-skim
   mozzarella cheese, cut into pieces or sliced

12 ounces cheddar cheese,
   cut into pieces or sliced

1 cup Panko Crumb Topping (recipe follows),
   plus more for garnish if desired

1. In a small saucepan, melt the butter over medium heat. Stir in the onion, garlic, salt, black pepper, cayenne, and paprika and cook for 3 minutes or until the onion is soft and translucent. Stir in the flour and cook for 1 minute longer. Whisk in the milk, bring to a simmer, and cook for 10 minutes. Then remove the pan from the heat.

2. Combine the macaroni with the fresh mozzarella, packaged mozzarella, and two-thirds of the cheddar in a multi-cooker. Add the milk mixture and stir to combine. Close the lid and set the machine to the "slow cook" program for 3 hours. Stir the mixture midway through.

3. Ten minutes before the end of the cooking time, top the macaroni and cheese with the remaining cheddar and the Panko Crumb Topping and replace the lid.

4. Serve the macaroni and cheese with additional Panko Crumb Topping if desired.

Panko Crumb Topping 2 cups

2 tablespoons unsalted butter

2 cups panko breadcrumbs

¼ teaspoon salt

Melt the butter in a small nonstick skillet over medium heat. Add the panko crumbs and salt, and cook, stirring constantly, until the crumbs are browned and crisp, about 5 minutes.

Candied Sweet Potatoes

This is almost a sweet potato galette. The thin slices of potato are arranged in a circular fashion and stacked in the bowl of the multi-cooker, each layer drizzled with a creamy syrup. Once the potatoes are cooked and slightly cooled, you can turn them out onto a plate and then garnish them with melted marshmallows. The resulting dish not only tastes amazing but is a showstopper to boot.

8 tablespoons (1 stick) plus 1 tablespoon unsalted butter

½ cup packed light brown sugar

¼ cup heavy cream

2 tablespoons cane syrup or molasses

1 teaspoon ground cinnamon

½ teaspoon salt

¼ teaspoon freshly grated nutmeg

¼ teaspoon ground ginger

⅛ teaspoon ground allspice

4 pounds sweet potatoes, peeled and cut into ¼-inch-thick slices on a mandoline

2½ cups mini-marshmallows

1 cup pecans, toasted (see page 66) and roughly chopped

1. In a small saucepan, combine the 8 tablespoons butter, brown sugar, heavy cream, cane syrup, cinnamon, salt, nutmeg, ginger, and allspice. Bring to a boil over medium heat, and stir until the sugar dissolves. Remove from the heat and set aside.

2. Shingle a single layer of sweet potatoes in the bottom of a multi-cooker bowl, and pour ¼ cup of the butter-sugar mixture on top. Continue to shingle layers of the potatoes and the sugar mixture until you have used it all. Close the lid of the multi-cooker, set it to the "steam" program, and cook for 1 hour.

3. In a small saucepan, heat the remaining 1 tablespoon butter, and when it has melted, add the marshmallows and cook over low heat until melted. Add the pecans and toss well.

4. Allow the potatoes to cool slightly. Remove the bowl of the multi-cooker from the machine. Invert a plate or platter over the top of the bowl, and carefully but quickly invert the bowl and plate together. The candied sweet potatoes should come out in one piece onto the plate, resembling a potato galette. Pour the marshmallow-pecan mixture over the top of the sweet potatoes, and serve immediately.

Steamed Mussels with Fennel and Hot Italian Sausage

One of my favorite Italian restaurants in Providence, Rhode Island, serves mussels prepared in a manner similar to this. This dish was created because I had a craving for it and couldn't get to Rhode Island. Simply put, it is mouthwateringly delicious.

3 tablespoons olive oil

8 ounces fresh hot Italian sausage, in bulk or removed from casings

1 cup diced fennel (about 1 medium bulb, small dice)

1 medium yellow onion, cut into small dice

2 tablespoons minced garlic (4 to 5 large cloves)

1 cup Herbsaint, Pernod, or pastis

1 cup homemade chicken stock (see page 5), packaged low-sodium chicken broth, water, or bottled clam juice

⅓ cup heavy cream

1 cup cherry tomatoes, halved

2 tablespoons chopped fresh parsley leaves

2 tablespoons chopped fresh fennel fronds

2 pounds mussels, rinsed

Salt and freshly ground black pepper

1 tablespoon chiffonade of fresh basil leaves

1 loaf crusty bread, warmed, for serving

1. Set a multi-cooker to the "white rice" program, and when it is hot, add the oil. Working in batches, brown the sausage, about 6 minutes per batch. Using a slotted spoon, transfer the cooked sausage to a plate. Add the fennel, onion, and garlic to the multi-cooker and cook until the vegetables are soft, about 7 minutes. Add the Herbsaint, chicken stock, and heavy cream, close the lid, and cook for 10 minutes.

2. Stir in the cherry tomatoes, parsley, and fennel fronds. Return the sausage to the multi-cooker. Add the mussels to the steamer basket, place it in the multi-cooker, close the lid, and set it to the "steam" program. Cook for 15 minutes.

3. Transfer the mussels from the steamer basket to the vegetable-sausage mixture, and stir. Cook for 2 minutes with the lid open, and then season with salt and pepper to taste. Garnish the mussels with the basil chiffonade and serve with warm crusty bread.

102 Emeril's Cooking with Power

Turkey Meatballs

You might think that there's no way that turkey meatballs could taste anywhere near as good as the old-fashioned beef kind. I'm here to tell you that they not only taste great, they're lighter and leaner, too!

2 slices whole wheat bread, crusts removed
⅓ cup buttermilk (see Note)
1 medium yellow onion, minced
½ cup finely diced red bell pepper
    (about ½ medium pepper)
¼ cup finely grated Parmigiano-Reggiano
    cheese, plus more for sprinkling if desired
1 clove garlic, minced
2 tablespoons ketchup
1 tablespoon minced fresh parsley leaves
1 egg, lightly beaten
1 teaspoon salt
½ teaspoon freshly ground black pepper
1½ pounds ground turkey, preferably dark meat
2 tablespoons olive oil
2 cups Fresh Tomato Sauce (recipe follows) or
    your favorite tomato sauce
1 pound whole wheat pasta

1. Place the bread and buttermilk in a small bowl and set aside for 5 minutes. Then mash the bread with a fork to form a paste.

2. In a large bowl, combine the onion, red bell pepper, Parmesan, garlic, ketchup, parsley, egg, salt, and pepper, and mix well. Add the bread mixture and stir to combine. Add the turkey and mix gently but thoroughly to combine. Shape into meatballs, about 2 tablespoons each, and refrigerate briefly to firm up, about 15 minutes.

3. Set a multi-cooker to the "white rice" program. When it is hot, add 1 tablespoon of the olive oil. Working in batches, brown the turkey meatballs until they are golden brown on all sides, 6 to 7 minutes, adding more oil as needed. Add the tomato sauce, close the lid, and cook for 35 to 40 minutes.

4. While the meatballs are cooking, bring a large pot of salted water to a boil, add the pasta, and cook according to the package directions.

5. Serve the meatballs and sauce ladled over the pasta, garnished with extra Parmesan if desired.

NOTE: *If you don't have buttermilk on hand, you can make your own by adding 1 tablespoon distilled white vinegar to 1 cup whole milk. Stir to blend and then set aside until thickened and creamy, usually about 5 minutes.*

Fresh Tomato Sauce 1 quart

Make this simple multipurpose tomato sauce when tomatoes are in season and freeze it to preserve a taste of summer.

½ cup olive oil

1 medium yellow onion,
    cut into small dice

3 cloves garlic, minced

½ teaspoon crushed red pepper

½ cup vermouth or dry white wine

3 pounds heirloom tomatoes,
    stemmed and roughly chopped

1 bay leaf

¼ cup chopped fresh basil leaves

1 teaspoon chopped fresh oregano leaves

1 teaspoon chopped fresh thyme leaves

2 tablespoons heavy cream

2 tablespoons finely grated
    Parmigiano-Reggiano cheese

1. Set a multi-cooker to the "white rice" program and add the olive oil. When it is hot, add the onion, garlic, and crushed red pepper. Cook, stirring occasionally, until the onion is soft and has begun to caramelize, 6 to 8 minutes. Add the vermouth and cook until it is reduced by half, 3 to 4 minutes. Add the tomatoes, bay leaf, basil, oregano, and thyme. Close the lid and bring the sauce to a simmer. Cook until the tomatoes have melted into the sauce and it has thickened slightly, about 1 hour.

2. Remove the bay leaf, mix in the heavy cream and Parmesan, and turn off the multi-cooker. The sauce can be left slightly chunky or it can be pureed in a blender until smooth. The sauce can be used immediately, refrigerated for up to 2 weeks, or frozen for up to 3 months.

Pork Tenderloin with Spaghetti Squash and Green Peppercorn Cream Sauce

The spaghetti squash cooks double-decker style in the multi-cooker: one half simmers in liquid, the other half steams in the basket. Served with marinated pork tenderloin draped in cream sauce, it's a meal fit for a king.

Pork

2 pounds pork tenderloin, trimmed
5 tablespoons extra-virgin olive oil
2 teaspoons kosher salt
1 teaspoon freshly ground
    black pepper
1 teaspoon minced garlic
    (about 1 large clove)
1 tablespoon honey
1 tablespoon sherry vinegar
¼ cup chopped fresh parsley leaves

Spaghetti squash

1 spaghetti squash, halved and seeded
Kosher salt, to taste
Freshly ground black pepper, to taste
1½ cups homemade chicken stock
    (see page 5) or packaged low-sodium
    chicken broth
4 tablespoons (½ stick) unsalted butter
2 teaspoons sherry vinegar
2 tablespoons chopped fresh
    parsley leaves

Green peppercorn cream sauce

1 tablespoon unsalted butter
¼ cup minced shallot
    (about 1 medium shallot)
2 teaspoons minced garlic
    (about 2 large cloves)
½ cup dry white wine
1 cup heavy cream
1 teaspoon drained and crushed
    green peppercorns
1 teaspoon Dijon mustard
Kosher salt, to taste
Freshly ground black pepper,
    to taste
2 tablespoons chopped fresh parsley leaves

1. Marinate the pork: Slice the pork into eight medallions and place them in a resealable plastic bag or other container. Combine the olive oil, salt, black pepper, garlic, honey, sherry vinegar, and parsley in a small bowl. Add this marinade to the pork, seal the bag or cover the container, and set aside at room temperature for 1 hour or refrigerate for up to 4 hours.

2. Meanwhile, cook the spaghetti squash: Season the squash halves with salt and pepper. Add the chicken broth and butter to a multi-cooker and add 1 squash half, cut side down. Place the steamer basket in the multi-cooker and place the other

squash half in it, cut side down. Close the lid and set the machine to the "steam" program. After 45 minutes, test the squash halves by inserting the blade of a thin knife into the center; there should be little to no resistance. If necessary, continue to cook for up to 15 minutes longer.

3. Transfer the squash halves to a platter and set aside until cool enough to handle. Transfer the cooking liquid to a medium bowl and cover to keep warm. Using a fork, gently scrape the inside of the squash halves to make the "spaghetti," and add it to the bowl with the reserved cooking liquid. Add the sherry vinegar and parsley to the spaghetti squash, and toss gently. Cover and set aside in a warm place until ready to serve.

4. Reset the multi-cooker to the "steam" program and heat it for 5 minutes. Remove the pork from the marinade and add half the pork medallions to the multi-cooker. Cook for 3 to 4 minutes per side, until browned, remove from the cooker, and set aside. Repeat with the remaining pork.

5. To make the green peppercorn cream sauce, add the butter to the multi-cooker (still on the "steam" setting). When it has melted, add the shallot and garlic and cook, stirring, until soft, about 1 minute. Add the wine and simmer for 4 minutes. Add the cream, green peppercorns, and Dijon mustard, and simmer for 4 minutes more. Season to taste with salt and pepper.

6. Return the pork medallions to the multi-cooker, along with any accumulated juices. Close the lid and cook for 10 to 12 minutes, until the pork registers 140°F on an instant-read thermometer. Transfer the pork to a pan and tent it with foil to keep warm. Add the chopped parsley to the sauce and cook until it is thick and bubbly and has reached the desired consistency.

7. To serve, divide the spaghetti squash among four plates. Arrange 2 pork medallions on each plate, and top with the sauce. (Alternatively, you can serve the pork thinly sliced.)

Easy Steak Stir-Fry

Who would have thought that you could stir-fry in a multi-cooker! It's really every bit as fast and easy as using a sauté pan or a wok.

2 tablespoons vegetable oil

1 pound skirt steak, cut against the grain into thin strips

8 ounces French green beans (haricots verts), trimmed and cut into 2-inch pieces

1 red bell pepper, stemmed, seeded, and julienned

2 tablespoons minced garlic (4 to 5 large cloves)

2 tablespoons minced fresh ginger

2 tablespoons Asian fish sauce

2 teaspoons soy sauce

1 teaspoon light brown sugar

1 teaspoon dark Asian sesame oil

1 teaspoon chili garlic sauce

2 cups hot steamed rice, for serving

1. Set the multi-cooker to the "white rice" program, and when it is hot, add the vegetable oil. Working in batches, brown the steak on all sides, 2 to 3 minutes per batch. Transfer the steak to a platter, using a slotted spoon.

2. Add the green beans, bell pepper, garlic, and ginger to the multi-cooker, close the lid, and cook for 10 minutes.

3. Meanwhile, in a small bowl, combine the fish sauce, soy sauce, brown sugar, sesame oil, and chili garlic sauce and whisk well.

4. Return the steak to the multi-cooker, add the sauce, and cook for 5 minutes with the lid open, stirring occasionally.

5. Serve immediately with the cooked rice.

Coconut Cardamom Tapioca Pudding

Tapioca pudding is creamy, classic, delicious, and so simple to make in the multi-cooker. This version combines coconut milk and coconut water with cardamom to create a Thai-inspired dessert.

2 cups whole milk

One 13.5-ounce can coconut milk

2 cups coconut water (see Note)

¾ cup palm sugar

4 cardamom pods

½ vanilla bean, split

½ cup small pearl tapioca

2 tablespoons unsalted butter

1 tablespoon light brown sugar

2 bananas, peeled and cut into
   ½-inch-thick rounds

2 teaspoons sesame seeds

½ teaspoon freshly grated nutmeg

1. In a large saucepan, combine the whole milk, coconut milk, 1 cup of the coconut water, the palm sugar, cardamom pods, and vanilla bean. Bring to a simmer over medium heat. Remove from the heat and let steep for 10 to 15 minutes.

2. Pour the milk mixture into a multi-cooker. Add the tapioca and stir well. Set the machine on the "white rice" program and close the lid. Cook, stirring every 5 to 10 minutes, until the tapioca is tender, about 30 minutes total.

3. Add the remaining 1 cup coconut water to the tapioca and stir well. Turn off the machine and remove the bowl (the tapioca will stick to the bottom of the bowl if it is not immediately taken off the heat once it has finished cooking). Remove the vanilla bean.

4. Heat a medium saucepan over medium-high heat and add the butter. When the butter begins to bubble, add the brown sugar and stir until dissolved. Add the sliced bananas, sesame seeds, and nutmeg, and sauté until the bananas are golden on both sides, about 4 minutes.

5. Serve the tapioca at room temperature with the sautéed bananas on top.

NOTE: *We chose to use coconut water in this recipe for its flavor. It's widely available and can be found in your local grocery store. Look for a brand of coconut water that does not contain any added ingredients such as preservatives or added juice.*

Dulce de Leche Rice Pudding

Who can resist the deliciously sweet and creamy delicacy of dulce de leche?

1 cup long-grain white rice, rinsed

1 cup whole milk

Two 15-ounce cans evaporated milk

2 tablespoons sugar

2 tablespoons unsalted butter

1½ teaspoons finely grated orange zest

1 teaspoon vanilla extract

½ teaspoon salt

2 cups water

One 15-ounce can dulce de leche,
    such as La Lechera brand

1. Place the rice in a multi-cooker and stir in the milk, evaporated milk, sugar, butter, orange zest, vanilla, salt, and water.

2. Set the multi-cooker to the "white rice" program and close the lid. After 10 minutes of cooking, stir the rice. Repeat two more times, for a total of 30 minutes.

3. Once the rice is tender, turn off the machine. With the lid still closed, allow the excess liquid to settle into the rice, about 10 minutes. Then, working gently so as not to break up the grains, spoon the rice into a large mixing bowl and allow it to cool, undisturbed, for 10 minutes.

4. At full power, warm the dulce de leche in a small microwave-safe bowl for about 10 seconds. You want the dulce de leche to be the consistency of the thickest syrup. It will easily bubble over in the bowl, so time at your discretion until the desired consistency is reached.

5. Add 8 heaping tablespoonfuls of the dulce de leche to the rice, and stir gently to combine. It is okay if it is not mixed in uniformly. Serve the rice pudding immediately or chilled, with additional warmed dulce de leche as desired.

S'mores Pudding

Everybody loves s'mores—they're an all-American classic! This s'mores pudding, made with milk chocolate, is topped with ooey-gooey toasted marshmallows and crushed graham crackers. Your kids will love you for this one.

½ cup sugar
½ cup unsweetened cocoa powder
¼ cup cornstarch
⅛ teaspoon salt
4 cups whole milk
1½ teaspoons vanilla extract
8 ounces milk chocolate, chopped
2 tablespoons unsalted butter
1 cup roughly chopped graham crackers
12 to 18 large marshmallows

1. Sift the sugar, cocoa powder, cornstarch, and salt into a medium bowl. If there appear to be any lumps, sift until the lumps have disappeared. Pour the dry ingredients into a multi-cooker and whisk in the milk, vanilla, and chocolate. Set the multi-cooker to the "white rice" program and bring the mixture to a boil, whisking constantly. Cook uncovered, until the pudding begins to thicken, 3 to 5 minutes.

2. Remove the bowl from the multi-cooker. Working quickly, pour or spoon the pudding into six 4-ounce ramekins or cups. Allow them to set up in the refrigerator, about 2 hours. The puddings can be covered and refrigerated for up to 2 days.

3. Melt the butter in a medium sauté pan over medium heat. Add the graham cracker crumbles and toast for 2 to 3 minutes, or just until golden brown.

4. To toast the marshmallows, preheat the broiler. Place the marshmallows on a lightly greased baking sheet, and broil them for 30 seconds. Using tongs, carefully turn the marshmallows over and broil for another 15 seconds. Remove from the oven and set aside. (Alternatively, you can toast them over a gas burner; see Note.)

5. When you're ready to serve the pudding, spoon about 1 tablespoon of the toasted graham cracker crumbles on top of each serving. Place 2 or 3 toasted marshmallows on top of the graham crackers, and serve immediately.

NOTE: *To toast the marshmallows on a gas stove, place 2 or 3 marshmallows on each of six long wooden or metal skewers, far enough down so that they will not easily fall into the fire when roasting. Place the skewers of marshmallows close to the flame of a gas burner for a charred result, or hover them above it for a more golden brown. Turn the skewers slowly, cooking all sides of the marshmallows.*

Drunken Cherries

Make this jubilee-inspired dessert when cherries are in season and enjoy it over ice cream, spooned onto warm biscuits, or even over yogurt for breakfast. The hardest part is pitting the cherries!

2¼ pounds fresh dark cherries,
    pitted
1¼ cups sugar
¼ cup Kirschwasser
¼ cup ruby port
2 teaspoons freshly squeezed lemon juice
1½ tablespoons cornstarch
2 tablespoons cool water
1 tablespoon Grand Marnier

1. Add the cherries to a multi-cooker and toss with the sugar, Kirschwasser, port, and lemon juice. Allow them to macerate, stirring them occasionally, until the sugar has dissolved and the cherries have released their liquid, 15 to 20 minutes.

2. Set the multi-cooker to the "steam" program, close the lid, and cook for 10 minutes. Then open the lid and continue to cook until the cherries are just tender, about 10 minutes longer.

3. In a small bowl, stir the cornstarch and the cool water to form a smooth slurry. Stir the cornstarch slurry into the bubbling cherries and continue to cook, uncovered and stirring occasionally, until the sauce is glossy and has thickened enough to coat the back of a spoon and the cherries are soft, about 10 minutes.

4. Transfer the cherries to a heat-proof bowl, stir in the Grand Marnier, and set aside to cool slightly. Serve the cherries warm or cool.

Vanilla Bean Cheesecake

You're in for a real treat with this one, folks. The most difficult part is setting the cake pan in the multi-cooker because, depending on the size of your springform pan, it may not rest evenly on the bottom of your multi-cooker. We found that wrapping foil around the base of the pan so that it fits inside snugly did the trick. Another trick is to set the unfilled crust-lined pan inside the multi-cooker, then pour in the cheesecake batter. Since this cheesecake takes a little bit of prep time and is best after refrigerating overnight, it's a great candidate for a make-ahead dessert.

Crust

6 tablespoons (¾ stick) unsalted butter, melted
1 sleeve cinnamon graham crackers (about 9 crackers), or 1½ cups ground
3 tablespoons sugar

Filling

1 pound cream cheese, at room temperature
2 tablespoons all-purpose flour
¾ cup sugar
3 large eggs, at room temperature
¼ cup sour cream
1 vanilla bean, pod split open and seeds scraped out (reserve the pod for another use), or 1 teaspoon vanilla extract
7 cups hot water, or more if needed

1. Preheat the oven to 350°F. Using a pastry brush, generously grease the bottom and sides of a 7-inch springform pan with some of the melted butter.

2. To make the crust, add the graham crackers and sugar to a food processor and process into crumbs. While the machine is running, drizzle in the remaining melted butter. Turn off the machine, remove the blade, and stir the crumbs with a rubber spatula until the butter is uniformly distributed. (If using ground crumbs, simply use a rubber spatula to mix the crumbs with the sugar and the remaining melted butter in a bowl until combined.)

3. Transfer the crumbs to the prepared springform pan, and using the palm of your hand, flatten the crumbs onto the bottom, forming a flat, even crust. Bake in the oven for 10 minutes, and then transfer the pan to a wire rack to cool. Once the crust is cool, securely wrap the bottom of the pan with aluminum foil to prevent water from leaking into the cake while it is cooking.

4. To make the filling, add the cream cheese to the bowl of a standing electric mixer fitted with the paddle attachment, and mix on medium speed until smooth. Add the flour and sugar and mix for 1 minute longer. Add the eggs one at a time, beating after each addition and allowing each egg to become fully incorporated before adding another. Add the sour cream and vanilla seeds, and mix until combined. Transfer the filling to the prepared springform pan.

5. Add the hot water to a multi-cooker. Carefully set the cake pan in the multi-cooker so that the pan sits as flat as possible. The water should come within an inch of the top of the pan; add more water if necessary. Close the lid. Cook the cake on the "slow cook" program for 5 hours, or until the cake is set.

6. Carefully remove the springform pan from the multi-cooker and let it cool on a wire rack for 1 hour. Refrigerate the cake for at least 8 hours before serving.

7. Before serving, run a thin knife around the sides of the cake, and then carefully remove the sides of the springform pan. To slice the cake, heat a knife under hot running water, wipe it dry, and then cut the cake into the desired servings, wiping the knife after each cut.

The Pressure Cooker:
Everything's better under pressure

A Note on Pressure Cookers

All the recipes in this chapter were tested in the Emeril by T-fal Electric Pressure Cooker. It features pressure cooking on both "high pressure" and "low pressure" settings and also has "browning," "sauté," "simmer," and "keep warm" programs. If you have another brand of electric pressure cooker, you should easily be able to adapt these recipes to your cooker. I have noted the approximate cooking temperatures for the various programs of the Emeril Pressure Cooker below. This should allow you to compare them with the programs on your pressure cooker in order to make any adjustments to the recipes if necessary.

➤ LOW PRESSURE: Suitable for cooking poultry, fish, and delicate vegetables. Preserves more vitamins during cooking compared to High Pressure. Always used with the lid closed and locked.

➤ HIGH PRESSURE: Suitable for meats, poultry, frozen foods, and some vegetables. This is the quickest cooking program. Always used with the lid closed and locked.

➤ BROWNING: Suitable for browning foods before cooking. Preset to operate at 356°F and should be used only with the lid open.

➤ SAUTÉ: Suitable for sautéing in order to soften foods before cooking. Preset to operate at 284°F and should be used only with the lid open.

➤ SIMMER: Suitable for simmering sauces at the end of the cooking cycle or to finish off cooking after adding ingredients. Preset to operate at 356°F and should be used only with the lid open.

➤ KEEP WARM: Keeps foods warm upon the completion of cooking. Keep in mind that fragile foods might overcook if kept in the pressure cooker for too long on "keep warm."

If you're shopping for a pressure cooker, here are a few recommended features:

➤ Pressure-cooks on both high and low settings.

➤ Removable bowl for easy cleanup.

➤ A "sauté" or "browning" program that allows you to sauté right in the bowl.

➤ A "keep warm" setting so that you can serve directly from the cooker if desired.

➤ A pressure release valve that allows you to release the pressure and check the cooking progress.

Curried Pumpkin Soup

When pumpkin season comes around and farmers' markets are full of beautiful varieties of cooking pumpkins, make sure to try this soup. The hardest part is peeling the pumpkin. Once that's done and it's diced up, it cooks in 3 minutes! You can make this soup using either canned coconut milk or canned coconut cream. The coconut cream is a bit richer and thicker than coconut milk and gives the soup a stronger coconut flavor.

2 tablespoons ghee (see Note, page 84), clarified butter, or unsalted butter

1 large yellow onion, minced

1½ tablespoons minced fresh ginger

1 tablespoon minced garlic (2 to 3 large cloves)

2 fresh red Thai chiles, thinly sliced crosswise

2 teaspoons cumin seeds

2 teaspoons black mustard seeds

1 teaspoon ground turmeric

½ teaspoon curry powder

2 pounds peeled, seeded, and coarsely chopped cooking pumpkin, such as kuri, or butternut squash (1-inch pieces)

1 tablespoon plus 1 teaspoon kosher salt

One 13.5-ounce can unsweetened coconut milk or coconut cream

Freshly squeezed juice of 1 orange (about ⅓ cup)

2 tablespoons light brown sugar

3½ cups water

1 cup plain Greek-style yogurt

Grated zest of 1 lime

Fresh cilantro sprigs or coarsely chopped fresh cilantro leaves, for garnish

1. Set a 6-quart pressure cooker to the "browning" program and add the ghee, onion, ginger, garlic, chiles, cumin seeds, mustard seeds, turmeric, and curry powder. Cook, stirring occasionally, until the onion is very soft and the spices are fragrant, 4 to 6 minutes. Add the pumpkin, salt, coconut milk, orange juice, brown sugar, and water. Close and lock the lid, and set to "low pressure" for 3 minutes.

2. Once the cooking is complete, open the pressure release valve and allow the steam to escape. Unlock and carefully open the lid. The pumpkin should be very tender; if it is not, continue to cook under pressure for 1 minute longer. Stir well, and adjust the seasoning if necessary.

3. The soup can be served immediately or refrigerated and gently reheated up to 1 week later. It will thicken upon sitting.

4. When you are ready to serve the soup, combine the yogurt and lime zest in a small bowl. Serve the soup garnished with a dollop of the lime yogurt and a sprig or sprinkling of cilantro.

Pho Ga (Chicken Pho)

4 to 6 servings

Chicken noodle soup never tasted so good!

Southeast Asian broth

One 4-pound chicken, cut
    into quarters
3 pounds chicken backs, necks,
    or bones
2 small yellow onions, quartered
2 carrots
3 cloves garlic
One 1-inch piece fresh ginger
1 tablespoon coriander seeds, toasted
1 teaspoon black peppercorns
1 small cinnamon stick
2 whole cloves
1 whole star anise
¼ cup Vietnamese fish sauce, or to taste
1 tablespoon palm sugar, or to taste

Pho

6 ounces cellophane noodles
1 yellow onion, thinly sliced, submerged in a
    bowl of cold water
4 green onions, thinly sliced on the diagonal
2 heads baby bok choy, cut into bite-size pieces

For serving

Fresh mint sprigs
Fresh Thai basil sprigs
Fresh cilantro sprigs or thinly sliced fresh
    cilantro leaves
Lime wedges
Thinly sliced serrano peppers
Hoisin sauce
Sriracha sauce

1. To make the Southeast Asian broth, rinse the chicken quarters and the chicken parts or bones under cool running water. Place all the chicken in a 6-quart pressure cooker and add water to cover. Close and lock the lid, and set to "low pressure" for 3 minutes.

2. Open the pressure release valve, allow the steam to escape, and carefully unlock and open the lid. Drain the chicken in a colander, discarding the liquid, and rinse any remaining scum or residue off the chicken. Clean the bowl of the pressure cooker of any residue.

3. Return all the chicken to the pressure cooker and add 2 quarts of water. Add the onions, carrots, garlic, ginger, coriander, black peppercorns, cinnamon stick, cloves, and star anise. Close and lock the lid, and reset the pressure cooker to "low pressure" for 35 minutes.

4. While the broth is cooking, soak the cellophane noodles in hot water in a medium mixing bowl or saucepan for at least 20 minutes. Once the noodles are soft, drain them in a colander and set them aside until ready to use.

5. Strain the Southeast Asian broth through a fine-mesh sieve into a large pot. Remove the meat from the chicken, discarding the skin and bones, and set it aside. Discard the vegetables and aromatics. Add the fish sauce and palm sugar to the broth, adjusting to taste.

128 Emeril's Cooking with Power

6. Divide the noodles equally among individual bowls, and top them with the reserved chicken. Drain the yellow onion, and add onion slices and green onions to each bowl.

7. Heat the broth over medium-high heat, add the bok choy, and simmer gently for 5 minutes or until the broth is hot and the bok choy is tender. Ladle the broth over the ingredients in the bowls. Serve immediately, with the mint, basil, cilantro, lime wedges, serrano peppers, hoisin sauce, and Sriracha sauce alongside for guests to add to their bowls as desired.

Collard Greens with Smoked Turkey

In the South we love our collards, but you can certainly use any hearty green here or even a mix of greens—whichever ones you like best. As when cooking greens in a pot, you still have to add them in batches so that there's room for more as each previous addition wilts—you know how they shrink—but in the pressure cooker, they'll be done in a flash.

1 pound smoked turkey legs or wings

3 cups homemade chicken stock
   (see page 5) or packaged low-sodium
   chicken broth

5 pounds collard, mustard, or turnip greens,
   or a mixture, large stems removed,
   leaves rinsed and chopped

2 cups chopped yellow onion
   (about 2 medium onions)

6 large cloves garlic, thinly sliced

1 tablespoon Creole Seasoning (page 29)
   or Emeril's Original Essence

1 teaspoon salt

½ teaspoon cayenne pepper

3 tablespoons molasses,
   preferably dark or robust

¼ cup balsamic vinegar

1. Add the turkey legs and chicken stock to a 6-quart pressure cooker. Close and lock the lid, and set to "high pressure" for 60 minutes.

2. Open the pressure release valve and allow the steam to escape. Unlock and carefully open the lid. Transfer the turkey legs to a plate, and when they are cool enough to handle, discard the skin and bones.

3. Shred the turkey meat and return it to the pressure cooker. Fill the cooker with one-third of the greens and add the onion, garlic, Creole Seasoning, salt, cayenne, molasses, and balsamic vinegar. Close and lock the lid, and reset to "high pressure" for 5 minutes.

4. Release the pressure, unlock, and carefully open the lid. Add another third of the greens and reset to "high pressure" for 5 minutes.

5. Again release the pressure, unlock, and carefully open the lid. Add the remaining greens and reset to "high pressure" for 35 minutes. The greens should be very tender and the broth flavorful.

6. Stir the greens and serve hot.

German-Style Potato Salad

You want a 5-minute potato salad? Here it is. Actually, the potatoes cook in 5 but you really want this baby to sit a while to soak up all the flavors before serving. Got your attention, though!

2 cups homemade chicken stock
    (see page 5) or packaged low-sodium
    chicken broth
1 cup cider vinegar
½ cup extra-virgin olive oil
1 tablespoon Creole mustard or
    other whole-grain mustard
3 teaspoons kosher salt
8 ounces bacon strips, diced
2 cups chopped yellow onion
    (about 2 medium onions)
½ cup chopped celery (about 1 rib)
¼ cup minced garlic (8 to 10 large cloves)
¼ teaspoon cayenne pepper
1 teaspoon freshly ground black pepper
¼ teaspoon celery seeds
½ cup chopped fresh parsley leaves
¼ cup chopped fresh chives
4 pounds medium Red Bliss potatoes,
    sliced ½ inch thick

1. In a medium bowl, whisk together the chicken stock, vinegar, ¼ cup of the olive oil, the mustard, and 2 teaspoons of the salt.

2. Set a 6-quart pressure cooker to the "browning" program. Once it is hot, add the bacon and cook for 5 minutes, or until the fat has rendered. Stir in the onion, celery, garlic, cayenne, the remaining 1 teaspoon salt, the black pepper, and celery seeds, and cook for 5 minutes. Stir in half of the fresh herbs and set aside the other half for garnish. Turn off the pressure cooker. Transfer the bacon mixture to a small bowl.

3. Once the pressure cooker is cool enough to touch, arrange one-third of the potatoes in an overlapping circular pattern in it. Top with one-third of the bacon mixture. Repeat two more times. Add the chicken stock by pouring it along the sides of the potatoes so that you don't "wash off" the bacon mixture. Close and lock the lid, and set to "high pressure" for 5 minutes.

4. Open the pressure release valve and allow the steam to escape. Unlock and carefully open the lid. Top the potatoes with the remaining ¼ cup olive oil and the remaining herbs. Allow the potatoes to cool for at least 30 minutes to absorb all the flavors before serving.

Green Beans with Smoked Ham Hock

Slow-cooked home-style green beans are everybody's favorite, and we pull it off here in the pressure cooker. First we make a ham hock broth. Then, after shredding the tender meat and adding the beans, in 15 minutes we're there.

2 ham hocks (1 to 1½ pounds total)

3 cups homemade chicken stock
   (see page 5) or packaged low-sodium
   chicken broth

2 cups chopped yellow onion
   (about 2 medium onions)

2 tablespoons minced garlic
   (4 to 5 large cloves)

3 pounds green beans, ends trimmed

1 teaspoon salt

½ teaspoon freshly ground black pepper

½ teaspoon crushed red pepper

1 tablespoon extra-virgin olive oil

¼ cup chopped fresh parsley leaves

1. Add the ham hocks and chicken stock to a 6-quart pressure cooker. Close and lock the lid, and set it to "high pressure" for 60 minutes.

2. Open the pressure release valve and allow the steam to escape. Unlock and carefully open the lid. Transfer the hocks to a plate, and when they are cool enough to handle, discard the skin, fat, and bones. Shred the meat and return it to the pressure cooker. Add the onion, garlic, green beans, salt, black pepper, and crushed red pepper. Close and lock the lid, and re-set to "high pressure" for 15 minutes.

3. Release the pressure, unlock, and carefully open the lid. Stir in the olive oil and chopped parsley, and serve hot.

Root Vegetables with Horseradish-Tarragon Vinaigrette

Marinated root vegetables in the pressure cooker: 2 minutes and they're done! How's that for a unique side dish to wow everyone?

8 ounces turnips, halved and
    sliced ½-inch thick
1 bulb fennel, halved, cored,
    and sliced ½-inch thick
8 ounces parsnips, cut into
    ½-inch-thick rounds
8 ounces carrots, cut into ½-inch-thick rounds
1 bunch leeks, ends trimmed, dark green part
    discarded, rinsed carefully and cut into
    1-inch pieces
8 ounces Red Bliss potatoes, quartered
2 tablespoons unsalted butter

¼ cup homemade chicken stock
    (see page 5), packaged low-sodium
    chicken broth, or water
¼ teaspoon salt
¼ teaspoon freshly ground black pepper
Horseradish-Tarragon Vinaigrette
    (recipe follows)

1. Add the vegetables, butter, stock, salt, and pepper to a 6-quart pressure cooker. Close and lock the lid, and set to "low pressure" for 2 minutes.

2. Open the pressure release valve and allow the steam to escape. Unlock and carefully open the lid. Pour the Horseradish-Tarragon Vinaigrette over the vegetables. You can serve the vegetables immediately, but they are also good warm or at room temperature.

Horseradish-Tarragon Vinaigrette ¾ cup

2 tablespoons champagne vinegar
1 tablespoon honey
1 tablespoon minced garlic (2 to 3 cloves)
1 teaspoon Dijon mustard
¼ cup freshly grated horseradish, or 2
    tablespoons prepared horseradish
½ teaspoon salt
Freshly ground black pepper
½ cup vegetable oil
1 tablespoon extra-virgin olive oil

1 tablespoon chopped fresh tarragon leaves
1 tablespoon chopped fresh parsley leaves

Combine the vinegar, honey, garlic, mustard, horseradish, salt, and pepper to taste in a small bowl. While whisking vigorously, slowly drizzle in the vegetable oil to form an emulsion. Whisk in the olive oil, tarragon, and parsley. Set aside until ready to use, or cover and refrigerate for up to 3 days.

Conchiglie Rigate with Butternut Squash Sauce

The butternut squash provides a rich texture and a slightly sweet flavor for this sauce. Garnished with walnuts, sage, and crispy bacon, this is the perfect pasta dish to warm you up on a cool fall or winter evening.

6 ounces bacon strips, diced

2 cups minced yellow onion
(about 2 medium onions)

2 cloves garlic, minced

1 teaspoon minced fresh marjoram leaves

2 tablespoons unsalted butter

2½ pounds butternut squash,
diced

2 cups heavy cream

1 teaspoon salt

½ teaspoon freshly ground black pepper,
plus more for garnish if desired

¼ teaspoon freshly grated nutmeg

1 pound *conchiglie rigate* (a ridged shell-
shaped pasta) or penne pasta

½ cup freshly grated Parmigiano-Reggiano
cheese

½ cup walnuts, toasted (see page 66) and
roughly chopped

½ cup panko breadcrumbs, toasted

¼ cup chiffonade of fresh sage leaves

1. Set the pressure cooker to the "browning" setting and add the bacon. Cook, stirring frequently, until the bacon is crisp and has rendered most of its fat, 5 minutes. Using a slotted spoon, transfer the bacon to a paper-towel-lined plate and set aside.

2. Add the onion, garlic, and marjoram to the pressure cooker and cook, stirring, until softened, 3 to 4 minutes. Add the butter, and when it has melted, add the butternut squash and stir well to coat. Add the heavy cream, salt, pepper, and nutmeg and cook until the cream has reduced slightly and the sauce has a thick consistency, 5 to 7 minutes.

3. Close and lock the lid, and set to "low pressure" for 3 minutes.

4. Bring a large pot of salted water to a boil, add the pasta, and cook according to the package directions.

5. Open the pressure release valve, allow the steam to escape, and carefully unlock and open the lid. Gently ladle the butternut squash sauce over the pasta in a large serving bowl and gently mix together, being careful not to break up the squash. Add half the Parmesan and toss well. Serve the pasta immediately, garnished with the reserved bacon, the remaining Parmesan, and the walnuts, panko, and sage. Sprinkle with black pepper if desired.

Tunisian-Inspired Chickpeas

This exciting mix of flavors is a simplified version of the famous Tunisian dish *leblebi*. In Tunisia it is most often enjoyed for breakfast, served at small sidewalk stalls with the hustle and bustle of street life all around. I do think that this is a dish that benefits from homemade stock, since the cooking time is so quick. One thing is for sure: don't skip the olives, capers, eggs, and harissa—it's the mingling of all these flavors that makes this dish something special.

The chickpeas cook in a mere 15 to 20 minutes after soaking overnight—how is that for a time-saver?

Chickpeas

1 pound dried chickpeas
Pinch of baking soda
1 large onion, finely chopped
2 tablespoons minced garlic
1½ quarts homemade beef stock (see page 6)
    or packaged low-sodium beef broth
3 tablespoons tomato paste
3 tablespoons extra-virgin olive oil
2½ teaspoons kosher salt
1½ teaspoons ground cumin

For serving

8 large eggs
Kosher salt
3 cups bite-size pieces day-old crusty peasant
    bread (toast in the oven if fresh)
2 red bell peppers, roasted (see page 19) and
    finely diced
½ cup sliced pitted black olives,
    such as Kalamata
2 tablespoons nonpareil capers, drained
½ cup harissa, preferably homemade
    (recipe follows), thinned with water to
    drizzling consistency
Extra-virgin olive oil
Freshly ground black pepper
Ground cumin
8 lemon wedges

1. Place the chickpeas in a large bowl, add water to cover and the pinch of baking soda, and soak overnight.

2. Drain the chickpeas, discarding the soaking liquid, and add them to a pressure cooker along with the onion, garlic, and beef stock. Close and lock the lid, and set to "high pressure" for 15 minutes.

3. Open the pressure release valve and allow the steam to escape. Unlock and carefully open the lid. The chickpeas should be tender. If not, continue to cook under pressure in 2-minute increments until they are tender.

4. Set the pressure cooker to the "simmer" program. Add the tomato paste, olive oil, salt, and cumin and stir to combine. Cook, uncovered, until the flavors come together, about 20 minutes.

5. When ready to serve, fry the eggs according to your liking and season them with salt to taste. Place a few pieces of bread in the bottom of each soup bowl and ladle some of the chickpeas and broth over the bread. Sprinkle each serving with some of the roasted pepper, olives, and capers.

6. Top each bowl with a fried egg and drizzle with harissa to taste. Serve with a drizzle of olive oil, a sprinkling of black pepper and cumin, and a lemon wedge.

Homemade Harissa   about 1/2 cup

Though you can certainly purchase prepared harissa, we love the fresh, forward flavor of homemade.

1 tablespoon cumin seeds (see Notes)
1 tablespoon caraway seeds (see Notes)
4 ounces fresh red chiles, such as cayenne or
    red jalapeños, stemmed and seeded
    (see Notes)
4 cloves garlic, minced
½ teaspoon salt
3 to 4 tablespoons extra-virgin olive oil,
    plus more for storing the harissa

1. Heat a small skillet over medium-high heat. Add the cumin seeds and cook, stirring or tossing frequently, until aromatic, 30 seconds to 1 minute. Remove from the skillet and set aside in a small bowl to cool. Repeat with the caraway seeds, and set them aside to cool separately.

2. When the cumin seeds have cooled slightly, transfer them to a spice mill or a clean coffee grinder and process until finely ground. Return them to the small bowl and set aside. Repeat with the caraway seeds. Measure out 1½ teaspoons of the ground cumin and 1 teaspoon of the ground caraway, and transfer the ground spices to a mortar. (The remaining ground cumin and caraway can be used for other purposes.)

3. Place the chiles in a food processor and pulse until chopped.

4. Add the chopped chiles, garlic, salt, and 1 tablespoon of the olive oil to the mortar, and using a pestle, mash repeatedly to form a chunky paste, adding more oil as needed to form a uniform texture. Taste, and adjust the seasoning if necessary by adding more salt or oil. Transfer to an airtight container and top with a thin film of olive oil. Refrigerate until ready to serve, up to several weeks, or freeze, topped with olive oil, in small containers for up to 6 months.

NOTES: *If you prefer, or if you don't have whole cumin or caraway seeds on hand, simply use 1½ teaspoons ground cumin and 1 teaspoon ground caraway.*

We prefer the smooth texture of harissa when it's made without chile seeds, but if a rougher texture is desired, simply use the chiles with their seeds. Be forewarned that the heat level will escalate, however!

Navy Bean and Chicken Chili

4 to 6 servings

This chili takes its personality from navy beans, a variety of green chiles, and tender chicken breasts that are cooked just to the point of doneness, then shredded and stirred back in near the end of cooking. The result: a chili that stands out from the pack with moist, flavorful pieces of chicken in every bite.

Make sure to start this a day in advance since the beans need to soak overnight—or soak them during the day while you're at work and then throw this together for dinner in little time when you get home.

2 pounds boneless, skinless chicken breasts

1 tablespoon plus 1½ teaspoons kosher salt

3½ teaspoons ground cumin

2 teaspoons chili powder

3 tablespoons olive oil

2 yellow onions, minced (3 cups)

3 poblano chiles, stemmed, seeded, and minced (1½ cups)

2 serrano chiles, stemmed, seeded, and minced

½ large bunch or 1 small bunch cilantro, stems and leaves reserved separately and finely chopped

1 canned chipotle chile in adobo sauce, stem removed, minced

¼ cup minced garlic (8 to 10 cloves)

1 teaspoon dried Mexican oregano or regular oregano, crushed with your fingers

1 pound navy beans, soaked overnight and drained

5½ cups homemade chicken stock (see page 5) or packaged low-sodium chicken broth

One 4-ounce can chopped green chiles, with juices

1 tablespoon plus 1 teaspoon yellow cornmeal

Garnishes

Sour cream

Lime wedges

Minced red onion

Finely minced jalapeños

Grated Monterey Jack–cheddar cheese blend

1. Season the chicken with 1½ teaspoons of the salt, 1 teaspoon of the cumin, and 1 teaspoon of the chili powder.

2. Set a pressure cooker to the "browning" program and heat the olive oil. When it is hot, add the chicken breasts (in batches if necessary) and cook until they are golden on both sides and just cooked through, 8 to 10 minutes. Transfer the chicken to a plate, tent it with foil or plastic wrap, and set aside.

3. Add the onions, poblano and serrano chiles, cilantro stems, chipotle chile, garlic, oregano, remaining 2½ teaspoons cumin, and remaining 1 teaspoon chili powder to the pressure cooker. Cook, stirring occasionally, until the vegetables are soft, 5 to 6 minutes. Add the beans, chicken stock, and canned chiles. Close and lock the lid, and set to "high pressure" for 15 minutes.

4. While the beans are cooking, shred the cooled chicken into bite-size pieces and set it aside.

5. Open the pressure release valve and allow the steam to escape. Unlock and carefully open the lid. Add the remaining 1 tablespoon salt and the cornmeal, and stir to combine. Close and lock the lid, and reset to "high pressure" for 8 minutes.

6. Release the pressure, unlock, and carefully open the lid. The beans should be tender; if not, continue to cook them under pressure for 1 to 2 minutes longer.

7. Set the pressure cooker to the "simmer" program. Stir in the chicken and cook, uncovered, until the chicken is heated through, about 10 minutes.

8. Serve the chili in bowls, garnished with sour cream, lime wedges, minced red onion, minced jalapeños, grated cheese, and cilantro leaves.

Chicken and Onions Braised in a Creamy Wine Sauce

This French-inspired dish tastes deceptively complex—but the simple preparation and super-quick cooking will leave you with time to spare. Serve this with hot crusty bread or over white rice or buttered noodles and be transported to the French countryside in your own home.

4 tablespoons olive oil

2½ pounds sweet onions, halved and sliced crosswise

2½ teaspoons kosher salt

3 ounces prosciutto or other salty ham, finely chopped

1 tablespoon minced garlic (2 to 3 cloves)

¾ cup dry white wine

¼ cup brandy

3 pounds boneless, skinless chicken thighs

1¼ teaspoons freshly ground black pepper

4 to 6 sprigs fresh thyme

1¼ cups heavy cream

2 tablespoons unsalted butter, at room temperature

3 tablespoons all-purpose flour

2 tablespoons coarsely chopped fresh parsley leaves

Warm crusty bread, hot steamed rice, or hot cooked noodles, for serving

1. Heat 2 tablespoons of the olive oil in a 6-quart pressure cooker set on the "browning" program. When it is hot, add the onions and ½ teaspoon of the salt and cook, stirring occasionally, until the onions are soft and tender and most of their liquid has evaporated, about 20 minutes. Add the prosciutto and garlic and cook for 2 minutes. Then add the white wine and brandy, stir, and transfer to a heat-proof mixing bowl.

2. Season the chicken thighs with 1½ teaspoons of the remaining salt and ¾ teaspoon of the pepper. Add the remaining 2 tablespoons olive oil to the pressure cooker (still on the "browning" program) and brown half of the thighs until golden on both sides, 8 to 10 minutes. Transfer them to a plate and brown the remaining thighs. When the second batch of thighs is golden, top them with half of the reserved onion mixture. Place the remaining reserved browned thighs on top of the onions, and spoon the remaining onion mixture over the top. Add the thyme sprigs and drizzle the cream over all. Close and lock the lid, and set to "low pressure" for 15 minutes.

3. Open the pressure release valve, allow the steam to escape, and carefully unlock and open the lid. The thighs should be very tender. Remove and discard the thyme sprigs. Transfer the thighs to a serving bowl and tent it with aluminum foil to keep warm.

4. Reset the pressure cooker to the "browning" program. In a medium heat-proof mixing bowl, mix the butter and flour to form a smooth paste. Spoon about 1 cup of the hot onion sauce from the pressure cooker into the butter-flour mixture and whisk to blend. Then stir the mixture into the remaining sauce in the pressure cooker, and add the remaining ½ teaspoon salt and remaining ½ teaspoon pepper. Cook, stirring occasionally, until the sauce is thickened and smooth, 10 to 15 minutes. Stir in the parsley and adjust the seasoning if necessary. Return the chicken thighs to the hot sauce to rewarm briefly before serving with hot bread, rice, or noodles.

Chicken Marsala

With modern pressure cookers, you can really do this dish well: brown the chicken on one side for color, then cook it under low pressure. Quick and perfectly delicious.

Four 8-ounce boneless, skinless chicken breasts
1¼ teaspoons salt
¾ teaspoon freshly ground black pepper
4 tablespoons (½ stick) unsalted butter
1 cup sliced yellow onion (about 1 medium onion)
1 sprig fresh thyme, plus 2 teaspoons fresh thyme leaves
12 ounces mushrooms, such as shiitake or button, wiped clean, stemmed, and sliced
2 teaspoons minced garlic (2 to 3 cloves)
3 tablespoons all-purpose flour
¾ cup Marsala
1½ cups homemade chicken stock (see page 5) or packaged low-sodium chicken broth
Hot cooked penne or your favorite pasta, for serving

1. Season the chicken all over with 1 teaspoon of the salt and ½ teaspoon of the pepper.

2. Set a 6-quart pressure cooker to the "browning" program and add 1 tablespoon of the butter. When the butter has melted, brown the chicken, in batches, on one side for 5 minutes. Remove the chicken and set aside.

3. Add the remaining 3 tablespoons butter to the pressure cooker. When it has melted, add the onion and thyme sprig, and cook until the onion is soft, about 3 minutes. Then add the mushrooms and cook for 5 minutes, until browned. Stir in the garlic, the remaining ¼ teaspoon salt, and the remaining ¼ teaspoon pepper. Stir in the flour and continue to cook, stirring as needed, for 2 minutes. Add the Marsala, simmer for 3 minutes, and then add the chicken stock. Return the chicken breasts to the pressure cooker, browned side up. Close and lock the lid, and set to "low pressure" for 2 minutes.

4. Bring a large pot of salted water to a boil, add the pasta, and cook according to the package directions.

5. Open the pressure release valve and allow the steam to escape. Unlock and carefully open the lid. Transfer the chicken to a serving platter. Discard the thyme sprig. Set the pressure cooker to the "simmer" program and reduce the sauce until the desired consistency is reached, about 3 minutes. Stir in the thyme leaves. Serve the Chicken Marsala over the pasta.

Cornish Hens with Apples and Cider

This dish is simple enough for a Sunday dinner and spectacular enough for a dinner party. The pan sauce, made with a slightly sweet Riesling wine and heavy cream, pairs well with apples, parsnips, and celery root. But feel free to use any root vegetables you like; my test kitchen has even made this dish with rutabaga and turnips and the results were every bit as good.

4 tablespoons (½ stick) unsalted butter
2 Cornish hens, cut in half, backbone removed
2 teaspoons sea salt
½ teaspoon freshly ground black pepper
½ cup thinly sliced shallot
    (about 2 medium shallots)
3 tablespoons all-purpose flour
¾ cup Riesling wine
¾ cup heavy cream
½ cup apple cider
2 tablespoons Calvados, applejack, or brandy
1 medium celery root,
    cut into ½-inch-thick wedges
    (about 2 cups)
4 parsnips, cut on the diagonal into
    ½-inch pieces (about 2 cups)
2 apples, peeled, cored, and cut into
    ½-inch-thick wedges
2 sprigs fresh thyme
Crusty bread, for serving

1. Add the butter to a 6-quart pressure cooker and set it to the "browning" program. Season the Cornish hens with the salt and pepper. When the butter begins to bubble and the pressure cooker is hot, brown the hens in batches, 3 minutes per side. Transfer the hens to a platter and tent it with aluminum foil to keep warm.

2. Add the shallot to the pressure cooker and cook for 3 minutes. Add the flour and cook for 2 to 3 minutes, just until the flour turns a golden brown. Whisk in the Riesling, cream, apple cider, and Calvados and cook for 6 to 8 minutes, until the sauce is reduced and slightly thickened. Return the hens, and any pan juices that may have accumulated, to the pressure cooker. Add the celery root and parsnips. Close and lock the lid, and set to "high pressure" for 12 minutes.

3. Open the pressure release valve, allow the steam to escape, and carefully unlock and open the lid. Add the apples and thyme sprigs, and cook on "high pressure" for 3 minutes.

4. Remove the thyme sprigs. Serve the Cornish hens with the sauce, vegetables, and apples spooned over them, and with crusty bread alongside.

Pressure Cooker Posole

4 quarts, about 8 servings

Classic posole cooks for most of the day and sometimes into the night. This is a scaled-down version that takes just a few hours. I will often make a batch of posole just to throw in the freezer so that it's on hand when the gang shows up at my house to watch the game on Sundays. I haven't had any complaints yet. Or any leftovers!

1 pound dried hominy (see Note)
2½ pounds boneless pork shoulder,
    cut into large chunks
1½ tablespoons salt
1 teaspoon hot Mexican-style red chili powder
    or regular chili powder (Mexican is spicier)
1 teaspoon freshly ground black pepper
2 tablespoons olive oil
4 cups chopped yellow onion
    (about 3 medium onions)
1 head garlic, separated into cloves, thinly sliced
One 14.5-ounce can diced tomatoes
1 ounce ancho chiles, stemmed, seeded, and
    chopped
1 ounce guajillo chiles, stemmed, seeded, and
    chopped
1 bay leaf
4 cups homemade chicken stock (see page 5)
    or packaged low-sodium chicken broth
1 cup diced Anaheim or Hatch chiles
½ teaspoon dried Mexican oregano or regular
    oregano
4 cups water
Tomatillo and Avocado Salsa (recipe follows)
Sour cream, for serving
Tortilla chips, for serving
Fresh cilantro leaves, for serving

1. Soak the hominy in cold water to cover for at least 2 hours or up to overnight.

2. Season the pork with 1 tablespoon of the salt, the chili powder, and black pepper.

3. Set a 6-quart pressure cooker to the "browning" program and add 1 tablespoon of the olive oil. Working in batches, brown the pork on all sides, 4 to 5 minutes per batch. Transfer the pork to a plate as it is browned.

4. Add the remaining 1 tablespoon olive oil to the pressure cooker and add 3 cups of the onion and the garlic. Cook until the onion begins to caramelize, 4 to 5 minutes. Add the diced tomatoes and cook for 2 minutes. Place the ancho and guajillo chiles on a large piece of cheesecloth, add the remaining 1 cup onions and the bay leaf, bring the edges together, and tie tightly with kitchen twine. Add to the pressure cooker.

5. Drain the hominy, discarding the liquid, and add it to the pressure cooker along with the chicken stock, Anaheim chile, oregano, remaining ½ tablespoon salt, and the water.

6. Close and lock the lid, and set to "high pressure" for 90 minutes.

7. Open the pressure release valve and allow the steam to escape. Unlock and carefully open the lid. Transfer the cheesecloth bag to a bowl and set it aside to cool. Once the bag is cool enough to handle, remove the chiles and onion and place them in a blender along with ½ cup of the cooking liquid (discard the bay leaf). Puree on high speed until smooth. Set this red chile sauce aside until ready to use.

8. Transfer the pork from the pressure cooker to a mixing bowl or a platter, and using two forks, shred the meat.

9. Return the pork to the pressure cooker and add ½ cup of the red chile sauce (extra sauce can be stored in an airtight container in the refrigerator for up to 3 weeks). The posole should look hearty but still be brothy enough to be thought of as a soup or a stew. Keep warm until ready to serve.

10. Serve the posole in bowls, garnished with the Tomatillo and Avocado Salsa, sour cream, tortilla chips, and cilantro leaves.

NOTE: *Dried hominy is a specialty item and can usually be found in Mexican markets and sometimes on the international aisle of your local grocery store, or ordered from Rancho Gordo, which is where we usually buy our hominy. Canned hominy is not a great substitute for dried because it is lacking in flavor and has a different texture. Visit RanchoGordo.com or Amazon.com for dried hominy if it is unavailable in your area.*

Tomatillo and Avocado Salsa   3 cups

This bright, tangy salsa is the perfect complement to the hearty posole, and if you happen to have any left over, serve it up with tortilla chips or over enchiladas and make some friends.

3 cups husked and diced tomatillos (small dice)
2 avocados, peeled, pitted, and cut into small dice
1 medium red onion, cut into small dice
1 cup diced poblano or Hatch chile (small dice)
¼ cup diced red jalapeño (small dice)
1 tablespoon minced garlic (2 to 3 large cloves)

2 teaspoons kosher salt
¼ teaspoon cayenne pepper
¼ cup freshly squeezed lime juice
¼ cup grapeseed or avocado oil
¼ cup chopped fresh cilantro leaves

1. Combine all the ingredients in a large bowl and mix well. Let stand at room temperature for at least 1 hour before serving.

2. The salsa can be stored in an airtight container in the refrigerator for up to 2 days.

Cajun-Style Pork with Turnips

6 servings

This hearty stew is often found on dinner tables in Cajun country during the butchering season. In case you don't happen to know already, pork and turnips are a terrific pairing and when stewed together and served over hot white rice, make for a very delicious and comforting meal. The pork takes on a terrific flavor after sitting overnight in the fridge, slathered with Creole seasoning and other Cajun spices. Do the prep the night before you plan to serve it, and then when you get to cooking, it can be on your dinner table in less than an hour.

2 pounds 3-inch cubes boneless Boston butt or pork shoulder

2 tablespoons Creole Seasoning (page 29) or Emeril's Original Essence

2 tablespoons minced garlic (4 to 6 cloves)

1 teaspoon sweet paprika

1 teaspoon freshly ground black pepper

2 teaspoons kosher salt, plus more for seasoning if needed

½ teaspoon cayenne pepper

½ cup plus 3 tablespoons vegetable oil

¾ cup all-purpose flour

1 large yellow onion, chopped

¾ cup chopped red or green bell pepper (about ½ medium pepper)

2 fresh hot red chiles, such as Tabasco, cayenne, or Thai bird, minced or thinly sliced, with seeds

4 cups homemade beef stock (see page 6) or packaged low-sodium beef broth

2½ pounds medium turnips (about 6), cut into 1-inch wedges

⅓ cup chopped green onion, both white and green parts (2 to 3 green onions)

2 tablespoons minced fresh parsley leaves

Hot steamed white rice, for serving

1. In a large bowl, season the pork with the Creole Seasoning, 1 tablespoon of the garlic, the paprika, black pepper, 1 teaspoon of the salt, and the cayenne. Add the 3 tablespoons oil and mix until the meat is evenly coated with the spices and oil. Cover the bowl with plastic wrap and refrigerate for at least 4 hours and up to overnight.

2. When you're ready to cook the stew, remove the meat from the refrigerator and allow it to come to room temperature for 30 minutes.

3. Place the flour in a resealable plastic food storage bag. Working in batches, add the meat and shake until completely coated with the flour.

4. Set a 6-quart pressure cooker to the "browning" program and add ¼ cup of

the remaining vegetable oil. Working in batches, brown the pork well on all sides, 4 to 6 minutes per batch, adding the remaining ¼ cup oil as needed. Transfer the pork to a bowl as it is browned.

5. Once all the pork has been browned, add the onion, bell pepper, and chiles to the pressure cooker and cook, stirring, until the vegetables are very soft and the floury drippings from the pork are golden brown, about 6 minutes. Add the remaining 1 tablespoon garlic and cook until fragrant.

6. Return the meat to the pressure cooker and add the beef stock. Close and lock the lid, and set it to "high pressure" for 30 minutes.

7. Open the pressure release valve, allow the steam to escape, and carefully unlock and open the lid. Check the meat—it should be very tender. Add the remaining 1 teaspoon salt and the turnips, pushing them down into the gravy. Close and lock the lid, and reset to "high pressure" for 10 minutes. The turnips should be fork-tender; if not, cook them under pressure for another 1 to 2 minutes.

8. Gently stir in the green onions and parsley, and adjust the seasoning if necessary. Serve the stew over hot white rice.

Pulled Pork with Classic Coleslaw

Pulled pork is a sure crowd-pleaser, especially when you pair it with Southwestern spices and cool, creamy coleslaw. Serve this dish at your next football party or tailgate and you'll have more fans than you know what to do with. The pork is coated with an intensely flavored rub and then refrigerated overnight before cooking. The results? Oh, baby.

Pulled pork

2 tablespoons light brown sugar
1½ tablespoons pimentón picante (hot smoked Spanish paprika)
1 tablespoon ancho chile powder
2 teaspoons hot Mexican-style chili powder or regular chili powder (New Mexican is spicier)
1 teaspoon dried Mexican oregano or regular oregano
1 teaspoon ground cumin
1 teaspoon ground coriander
1 teaspoon freshly ground black pepper
One 5-pound bone-in pork shoulder, cut into large chunks
2 teaspoons salt
2 tablespoons grapeseed oil
1 yellow onion, minced
4 cloves garlic, sliced
4 cups homemade chicken stock (see page 5) or packaged low-sodium chicken broth

Coleslaw

½ cup buttermilk (see Note, page 105)
½ cup mayonnaise
2 tablespoons Dijon mustard
2 tablespoons cider vinegar
½ teaspoon celery seeds
1½ teaspoons salt
¼ teaspoon cayenne pepper
1 small head red cabbage, thinly sliced
1 small head napa cabbage, thinly sliced
2 carrots, thinly sliced on a mandoline or shaved with a vegetable peeler

For serving

1 head butter lettuce
Tortilla chips, broken into bite-size pieces
Lime wedges

1. Marinate the pork: In a large bowl, combine the brown sugar, pimentón, ancho chile powder, hot chili powder, oregano, cumin, coriander, and black pepper, and mix well. Place the pork in the bowl and toss with the spice mix, coating all sides of the pork. Cover with plastic wrap or transfer to a resealable plastic bag, and refrigerate overnight.

2. Let the pork come to room temperature before cooking. Season the pork with the salt.

3. Set a pressure cooker to the "browning" program and add the grapeseed oil. When

the oil is hot, brown the pork, working in batches, about 5 minutes per batch. As it is browned, transfer the pork to a baking sheet and set it aside. Add the onion and garlic to the pressure cooker and cook for 2 to 3 minutes. Return the pork to the pressure cooker and add the chicken stock. Close and lock the lid, and set to "high pressure" for 60 minutes.

4. Open the pressure release valve and allow the steam to escape. Unlock and carefully open the lid. The pork should be fork-tender; if not, cook it under pressure for another 10 minutes. Once it is done, transfer the pork to a platter and let it rest until it is cool enough to handle.

5. Shred the pork with two forks and return it to the broth. The pork can be served at this point or frozen for up to 3 months.

6. Prepare the coleslaw by combining the buttermilk, mayonnaise, mustard, vinegar, celery seeds, salt, and cayenne pepper in a large bowl and mixing well. Add the cabbage and carrots and toss well. Set aside for at least 15 to 20 minutes. The salad can be made up to several hours in advance and refrigerated until ready to serve.

7. To serve the pork, separate the butter lettuce leaves and place them on a platter. Top the leaves with the warm pulled pork, place some of the coleslaw on top of the pork, and top with the tortilla chips. Serve with lime wedges.

Cannellini Bean Stew

This deliciously meaty bean stew gets its character from anchovies, tomatoes, and garlic (although it doesn't taste fishy at all). To round out the Tuscan flavors, I add basil, extra-virgin olive oil, and a splash of balsamic vinegar. Enjoy it with crusty bread.

1 pound dried cannellini or navy beans

12 ounces smoked sausage,
    cut into ½-inch-thick rounds

1½ pounds country-style pork ribs,
    meat cut into 1-inch chunks
    (reserve the bones if ribs are bone-in)

2 sprigs fresh rosemary

2 sprigs fresh thyme

1½ tablespoons fennel seeds

2 teaspoons kosher salt

1 teaspoon freshly ground black pepper

2 cups chopped yellow onion
    (about 2 medium onions)

10 cloves garlic, smashed

10 canned anchovy fillets

One 14.5-ounce can diced tomatoes, with juices

6 cups homemade chicken stock (see page 5) or
    packaged low-sodium chicken broth

1 cup chopped fresh basil leaves

1 tablespoon extra-virgin olive oil

1 tablespoon balsamic vinegar

1. Add the beans, sausage, pork, bones (if available), rosemary and thyme sprigs, fennel seeds, salt, pepper, onion, garlic, anchovies, tomatoes, and chicken stock to a 6-quart pressure cooker. Close and lock the lid, and set to "high pressure" for 90 minutes.

2. Open the pressure release valve, allow the steam to escape, and carefully unlock and open the lid.

3. Discard the bones (if necessary) and stir in the basil, olive oil, and balsamic vinegar. Serve hot.

Red Beans and Rice

In the time the beans are cooking, you can make cornbread, a salad, and fried chicken. Everybody will be happy, and you'll have meals for a week.

1 pound dried red kidney beans
2 smoked ham hocks
2 cups chopped yellow onion
    (about 2 medium onions)
1 cup chopped green bell pepper
    (about 1 small pepper)
1 cup chopped celery (2 ribs)
4 cloves garlic, smashed
2 bay leaves
2 teaspoons dried oregano
2 teaspoons dried thyme
1 tablespoon kosher salt
½ teaspoon crushed red pepper
One 14-ounce can diced tomatoes,
    with juices
1 pound smoked sausage,
    cut into ½-inch-thick rounds
7 cups water
Hot steamed white rice, for serving
Chopped green onion, for serving

1. Add all the ingredients except the rice and green onion to a pressure cooker. Close and lock the lid, and set to "high pressure" for 90 minutes.

2. Open the pressure release valve and allow the steam to escape. Unlock and carefully open the lid. Stir the beans; they will thicken as they sit.

3. Serve hot over rice, garnished with chopped green onion.

Lamb Stew with Israeli Couscous, Sweet Potatoes, and Preserved Lemon

This flavor combination is full of character, over the top, and truly delicious as is. If you'd like to add a sweet component, though, stir in a few golden raisins (up to ½ cup) while you're simmering the couscous.

2 pounds boneless lamb shank, leg, or shoulder, trimmed and cut into 1-inch chunks

2 tablespoons Creole Seasoning (page 29) or Emeril's Original Essence

3 tablespoons olive oil

1½ cups chopped yellow onion (about 1 large onion)

¼ cup minced garlic (8 to 10 cloves)

1 sprig fresh rosemary

1½ cups diced sweet potato (about 1 potato) or butternut squash

2 teaspoons salt

1 teaspoon freshly ground black pepper

1 cup dry red wine

4 cups homemade beef stock (see page 6) or packaged low-sodium beef broth

1 cup Israeli couscous

1 tablespoon minced preserved lemon or freshly squeezed lemon juice

½ cup chopped fresh parsley leaves

¼ cup chopped fresh mint leaves

Harissa, for serving, if desired (see page 142)

1. Season the lamb all over with the Creole Seasoning.

2. Set a 6-quart pressure cooker to the "browning" program, and heat 2 tablespoons of the olive oil. Working in batches, brown the lamb on all sides, about 5 minutes. Using a slotted spoon, transfer the lamb to a plate as it is browned.

3. Add the onion, garlic, rosemary, and sweet potato to the pressure cooker and cook, stirring as needed, for 5 minutes. Add the salt, pepper, red wine, and beef stock. Return the lamb to the pressure cooker. Close and lock the lid, and set to "high pressure" for 30 minutes.

4. While the lamb is cooking, heat the remaining 1 tablespoon olive oil in a large sauté pan over medium heat. Add the couscous and toast, stirring frequently, until it is lightly browned, about 5 minutes. Remove from the heat and set aside.

5. Open the pressure release valve and allow the stream to escape. Unlock and carefully open the lid. Set the pressure cooker to the "simmer" program and stir in the toasted couscous. Simmer the couscous until tender, about 15 minutes.

6. Stir in the preserved lemon and fresh herbs. Serve the stew warm, with harissa if desired.

Sunday Gravy

Many Italian-American families gather every Sunday to enjoy this spectacular, typically long-simmered sauce. It usually contains a number of different meats and sausages, meatballs, and sometimes even the stuffed, rolled, and tied meat known as *braciola*. In my simplified version here, I've gathered enough ingredients to make an intensely flavored sauce, but the best part is that what normally takes all day to cook is on the table in about 1½ hours. The end result? *Mamma mia*, you tell me!

¼ cup olive oil

1½ pounds boneless beef chuck roast, cut into 1-inch-thick slices

1½ pounds country-style pork ribs (bone-in or boneless—either is fine)

4 teaspoons kosher salt

1¼ teaspoons freshly ground black pepper

3 cups chopped yellow onion (about 2 large onions)

3 tablespoons tomato paste

3 tablespoons minced garlic (6 to 7 cloves)

¾ cup dry red wine

Two 28-ounce cans whole Italian-style tomatoes, crushed with your hands, with juices

¾ teaspoon crushed red pepper

2 bay leaves

3 tablespoons coarsely chopped fresh oregano leaves

1¼ pounds fresh sweet Italian sausage, in bulk or removed from casings, formed into 1½-inch meatballs

Hot cooked pasta, for serving

Freshly grated Pecorino Romano cheese, for serving

1. Set a pressure cooker to the "browning" program and heat the olive oil. Season the chuck roast and pork ribs on all sides with 3 teaspoons of the salt and 1 teaspoon of the black pepper. Working in batches, cook the meat until browned on both sides, 8 to 10 minutes per batch. As it is browned, transfer to a plate and set aside.

2. Add the onion to the pressure cooker and cook until it is very soft, about 6 minutes. Add the tomato paste and garlic and cook, stirring, for 2 to 3 minutes. Add the red wine and let it simmer for 2 minutes. Then return the browned meats to the pressure cooker and add the tomatoes and their juices, the remaining 1 teaspoon salt, remaining ¼ teaspoon black pepper, the crushed red pepper, bay leaves, and 1 tablespoon of the oregano. Close and lock the lid, and set to "high pressure" for 30 minutes.

3. Open the pressure release valve and allow the steam to escape. Unlock and carefully open the lid. Stir the sauce to keep it from sticking to the bottom. Close and lock the lid and re-set to "high pressure" for 30 minutes longer. The meats should be falling-apart tender. If not, cook under "high pressure" for 5 to 10 minutes more.

4. Set the pressure cooker to the "simmer" program and add the remaining 2 tablespoons oregano. Gently drop the sausage meatballs into the sauce. Cook, stirring gently after the first 10 minutes, until the sauce is thickened and the sausage meatballs are cooked through, about 20 minutes. The other long-cooked meats will fall apart into small pieces and melt into the sauce as you stir the meatballs—don't worry, this is how it's supposed to look! Remove and discard the bay leaves.

5. Bring a large pot of salted water to a boil, add the pasta, and cook according to the package directions.

6. Serve the sauce over the cooked pasta and garnish it with the Pecorino Romano.

7. The sauce will keep, refrigerated, for up to 1 week, or can be frozen for up to 6 months.

Quick Osso Buco

Who says veal shanks can't be meltingly tender in just over an hour? Check this out! Serve them over Risotto Milanese (page 20) for the classic match made in heaven or over the Creamy Polenta (page 96) for true comfort.

6 veal shanks (4 to 4½ pounds total), about 1½ inches thick, tied tightly around the middle with kitchen string

3¾ teaspoons kosher salt

2 teaspoons freshly ground black pepper

½ cup all-purpose flour

¼ cup olive oil

2½ cups chopped yellow onion (about 2 medium onions)

1 cup diced celery (2 to 3 ribs)

1 cup diced carrot (2 medium carrots)

3 tablespoons tomato paste

2 tablespoons minced garlic (4 to 6 cloves)

2 bay leaves

1 tablespoon chopped fresh thyme leaves

1 tablespoon chopped fresh rosemary leaves

1½ cups dry red wine

4½ cups rich veal stock, or homemade beef stock (see page 6), or substitute 1 cup demi-glace and 3½ cups packaged low-sodium beef broth

2 tablespoons unsalted butter, at room temperature

¼ cup chopped fresh parsley leaves

1. Season the meat on all sides with 2½ teaspoons of the salt and 1 teaspoon of the pepper. Dredge the veal shanks in the flour, shaking them to remove any excess. Set the shanks aside. Reserve 3 tablespoons of the remaining dredging flour and discard the rest.

2. Heat the olive oil in a 6-quart pressure cooker set to the "browning" program. Brown the shanks on all sides, in batches if necessary, 10 to 12 minutes per batch. Remove the shanks from the pressure cooker and set aside.

3. Add the onion, celery, and carrot to the pressure cooker and cook until softened and lightly browned around the edges, 4 to 6 minutes. Add the tomato paste, garlic, bay leaves, half of the thyme, half of the rosemary, the remaining 1¼ teaspoons salt, and the remaining 1 teaspoon pepper. Cook, stirring, for 2 minutes. Add the red wine, scraping the bottom of the pan to loosen any browned bits. Add the stock and return the shanks to the pressure cooker. Bring to a boil. Close and lock the lid, and set to "high pressure" for 65 minutes.

4. Open the pressure release valve and allow the steam to escape. Unlock and carefully open the lid. The shanks should be nearly fall-from-the-bone tender. If the meat still meets with resistance, continue to cook under pressure for 2 to 4 minutes longer.

Carefully transfer the shanks to a bowl and tent it with aluminum foil to keep warm. Remove and discard the bay leaves.

5. In a medium heat-proof bowl, mix the butter with the reserved dredging flour to form a smooth paste. Ladle 1 cup of the hot cooking liquid into the bowl and whisk to combine. Then stir this flour-broth mixture into the cooking liquid in the pressure cooker. Add the remaining rosemary and thyme. Set the pressure cooker to the "simmer" program and cook, stirring occasionally, until the sauce is thickened and smooth and any floury taste is gone, 5 to 10 minutes. Adjust the seasoning if necessary, then return the shanks to the sauce to rewarm briefly before serving. Serve as desired, garnished with a sprinkling of parsley.

Korean-Style Beef Stew

This is classic Korean comfort food. Don't be put off by the large ingredients list—most of these items may already be in your pantry or refrigerator. This is an easy dish to put together, and it takes only about an hour from start to finish. One of the best things about this stew is that it tastes even better the next day.

Marinade

4 cloves garlic, minced

3 stalks lemongrass, trimmed and thinly sliced

One 1-inch piece fresh ginger, grated

3 tablespoons reduced-sodium tamari

2 tablespoons canola oil

1 tablespoon chili garlic sauce

1 teaspoon dark Asian sesame oil

2 teaspoons light brown sugar

3½ pounds boneless beef chuck roast, cut into 2-inch cubes

Stew

2 tablespoons canola oil

¼ cup reduced-sodium tamari

2 tablespoons sugar

2 tablespoons sake

1 red onion, cut into ½-inch-thick wedges

2 carrots, cut ¼-inch thick on the diagonal

1 red bell pepper, stemmed, seeded, and cut into medium dice

2 tablespoons minced jalapeño

1 tablespoon roughly chopped garlic (2 to 3 cloves)

1 tablespoon grated fresh ginger

1 teaspoon salt

½ teaspoon Korean chile powder or crushed red pepper

4 cups homemade beef stock (see page 6) or packaged low-sodium beef broth (homemade stock is preferable)

1 head napa or savoy cabbage, cut into 1-inch squares (about 5 cups)

Garnish

1 cup mung bean sprouts

2 tablespoons sesame seeds, toasted

3 or 4 green onions, thinly sliced

Dark Asian sesame oil

For serving

Hot cooked Korean sweet potato noodles or steamed short-grain rice (see Note)

1. To make the marinade, combine the garlic, lemongrass, ginger, tamari, canola oil, chili garlic sauce, sesame oil, and brown sugar in a mini food processor or a blender, and process until the mixture resembles a paste.

2. In a large mixing bowl, toss the beef with the marinade until it is well coated. Cover and refrigerate for at least 1 hour or up to overnight.

3. When you are ready to cook, allow the beef to come to room temperature before proceeding.

4. To make the stew, add the oil to a 6-quart pressure cooker and set the machine to the "browning" program. When it is hot, add the beef, in batches, and cook, turning it occasionally, until it is evenly browned, about 5 minutes per batch. As it is browned, transfer the meat to a plate.

5. When all the meat is browned, add the tamari, sugar, and sake to the pressure cooker and simmer for 1 minute. Then add the onion, carrots, red bell pepper, jalapeño, garlic, ginger, salt, and chile powder and cook, stirring, until the vegetables have wilted, about 6 minutes. Return the browned meat to the pressure cooker and add the stock. Close and lock the lid, and set to "high pressure" for 15 minutes.

6. Open the pressure release valve, allow the steam to escape, and carefully unlock and open the lid. Add the cabbage, stir well, and replace the lid. Cook on "high pressure" for an additional 15 minutes.

7. Garnish the stew with the mung bean sprouts, sesame seeds, green onions, and a sprinkling of sesame oil. Serve over Korean sweet potato noodles or steamed rice.

NOTE: *Korean glass noodles or vermicelli are made from sweet potato starch. Thin, long, translucent, glass-like noodles with a chewy texture, they're similar to cellophane noodles but slightly thicker with a firmer bite. They're a must when making Korean food. You can buy Korean noodles at your local Asian market or order them online.*

Emeril's Fastest BBQ Brisket

Here's an easy, quick, and delicious way to satisfy even the biggest brisket aficionado. The pressure cooker does all the work and you enjoy all the benefits.

4½ pounds beef brisket,
    trimmed and quartered
3 tablespoons Worcestershire sauce
1 tablespoon sweet paprika
1 tablespoon dry mustard
1 teaspoon chili powder
4 tablespoons olive oil
2 teaspoons salt
1 medium yellow onion, diced
6 cloves garlic, sliced
One 12-ounce bottle lager beer
1 cup your favorite barbecue sauce
¼ cup light brown sugar
Slider buns, for serving
Classic Coleslaw (page 158)
    or your favorite coleslaw, for serving

1. Place the brisket in a large bowl, add the Worcestershire sauce, paprika, mustard, chili powder, and 2 tablespoons of the olive oil, and toss. Let the brisket marinate for 30 minutes at room temperature.

2. When ready to cook, season the beef with the salt.

3. Set a 6-quart pressure cooker to the "browning" program. When it is hot, add the remaining 2 tablespoons olive oil and brown the beef in batches. As it is browned, transfer the beef to a baking sheet and set aside.

4. When all the brisket is browned, add the onion and garlic to the pressure cooker and cook for 6 minutes, or until the onion is soft and slightly translucent. Return the beef to the pressure cooker and add the beer, barbecue sauce, and brown sugar. Close and lock the lid, and set to "high pressure" for 1½ hours.

5. Open the pressure release valve, allow the steam to escape, and carefully unlock and open the lid. Transfer the beef to a baking sheet, and when it is cool enough to handle, thinly slice it across the grain.

6. Set the pressure cooker to the "simmer" program. Return the beef and any accumulated juices to the cooker and cook for 15 to 20 minutes.

7. Serve the brisket on slider buns, topped with the coleslaw.

8. The brisket can be stored in an airtight container in the refrigerator for up to 3 days or frozen for up to 3 months.

Poached Pears

The color of these pears will vary according to the type of wine you use. The darker, stronger grapes from a wine such as a Cabernet will shade the pears a deeper purple than will a port or a lighter, fruitier red wine. Any wine you choose will give you delicious results.

3 cups Cabernet Sauvignon, other red wine, port, or a blend
¾ cup water
¾ cup plus 2 tablespoons sugar
1 vanilla bean, split
One 3-inch cinnamon stick
One 1-inch-wide strip of lemon zest
2 pounds firm-ripe red or green Anjou pears
1 teaspoon freshly squeezed lemon juice
1 cup heavy cream

1. Add the Cabernet Sauvignon, water, the ¾ cup sugar, the vanilla bean, cinnamon stick, and lemon zest to a 6-quart pressure cooker and whisk to dissolve the sugar. Peel the pears and add them to the pressure cooker. Close and lock the lid, and set to "high pressure" for 2 minutes.

2. Open the pressure release valve and allow the steam to escape. Unlock and carefully open the lid. Carefully remove the bowl from the pressure cooker. Cut a piece of parchment paper the diameter of the bowl and place it on top of the pears. Set a small plate on top of the paper to submerge the pears in the cooking liquid. Allow the pears to cool in the liquid. You can keep the pears in their liquid at room temperature until ready to serve, up to 8 hours, or they can be refrigerated in their liquid for up to 3 days.

3. Remove the pears from the liquid and set them aside. Scrape the vanilla seeds from their pod into the bowl, and discard the pod. Remove and discard the strip of lemon zest.

4. Return the bowl to the pressure cooker and set it to the "browning" program. Simmer the liquid for about 50 minutes, or until large bubbles are breaking along the surface and it has reduced to a syrupy consistency. Transfer the syrup to a heat-proof container and stir in the lemon juice. The sauce will continue to thicken as it cools. If it thickens too much, thin it with a little hot water.

5. Using a large whisk or an electric mixer, whip the cream with the remaining 2 tablespoons sugar in a medium bowl until stiff peaks form.

6. To serve, halve and core the pears, and top them with the syrup and whipped cream. (Alternatively, you can slice the pears into 1-inch-thick slices and arrange the slices on each plate. Drizzle some of the syrup over the pears and garnish with a dollop of whipped cream.)

Compote of Dried Berries and Walnuts

This compote is simple to put together and makes a wonderful topping for both sweet and savory dishes. It pairs well with waffles, pancakes, and biscuits, but you could also serve it with roasted turkey or pork tenderloin. I like to make this compote to give as a gift during the holidays. There's plenty to go around.

1 cup dried goji berries (see Note)
1 cup dried blueberries
1 cup dried sour cherries
1 cup dried raspberries
1 cup dried mulberries or strawberries
    (or dried apricots if you are unable
    to find the berries)
2½ cups freshly squeezed orange juice
¼ cup sugar
½ cup Framboise liqueur
1 teaspoon finely grated orange zest
⅛ teaspoon salt
1½ cups chopped toasted walnuts
    (see page 66)

1. Place all the ingredients except the walnuts in a 6-quart pressure cooker and stir to mix well. Close and lock the lid, and set to "high pressure" for 3 minutes.

2. Open the pressure release valve, allow the steam to escape, and carefully unlock and open the lid. Fold in the walnuts and allow to cool.

3. The compote can be stored in an airtight container in the refrigerator for up to 4 weeks.

> NOTE: *Goji berries, also known as wolf berries, are grown in the hills of Tibet and Mongolia. They are considered a super food because they are packed with antioxidants. You can buy goji berries at your local health food store or online.*

The Deep Fryer:

Straighten up and fry right

Hushpuppies

The Deep Fryer

A Note on Electric Deep Fryers

All the recipes in this chapter were tested in the Emeril by T-fal Deep Fryer. It has a near-4-quart oil capacity and is able to cook up to 2⅔ pounds of food per batch. Of course any electric deep fryer with multiple temperature settings will work for these recipes. If your fryer has temperature settings that are not variable, simply choose the temperature closest to our recommended frying temperature and adjust the cook times accordingly. We used vegetable oil for testing most of these recipes, but peanut oil would also work well, especially for the savory recipes.

Some things to look for when shopping for an electric deep fryer:

➤ Large capacity, so that cooking for a crowd is easily accomplished.

➤ Oil change indicator light, so there's no guesswork as to when to change the oil.

➤ Integrated oil filtration, to help you use oil longer by filtering it between uses.

➤ Dishwasher-safe parts, for easy cleanup.

➤ A built-in timer.

Chickpea Fries

Chickpea flour, with its toasty, nutty flavor, has long been enjoyed throughout the Mediterranean in the form of fritters and crêpes. In this case a simple chickpea batter is spread out on a baking sheet and then refrigerated for a few hours (this makes it easier to cut the fries into an even shape).

¼ cup plus 2 tablespoons olive oil
1½ cups chickpea flour
1½ tablespoons kosher salt, plus more for sprinkling
1½ teaspoons finely ground white pepper
1 cup whole milk
1 cup water
One 5.2-ounce package Garlic and Fine Herbs Boursin cheese
Vegetable oil, for deep-frying

1. Using 1 tablespoon of the olive oil, grease a 12 x 8-inch rimmed baking sheet. Place a sheet of waxed paper on top.

2. In a large saucepan, combine the chickpea flour with the salt and white pepper. Slowly drizzle the milk and water into the chickpea mixture, whisking constantly to form a smooth batter. Add the ¼ cup olive oil, and continue to whisk until fairly smooth. The batter will have some lumps. Heat the batter over medium-high heat and cook for 2 to 3 minutes, or until the batter thickens, whisking constantly. Add the Boursin cheese, switch to a wooden spoon, and beat the batter for 2 minutes, until the mixture is smooth and the cheese has completely melted.

3. Remove the pan from the heat and immediately transfer the batter to the prepared baking sheet. Using an offset spatula, smooth the top of the batter and gently press it to distribute it evenly. Oil a second sheet of waxed paper with the remaining tablespoon of olive oil and place it over the top. Wrap the whole thing tightly in plastic wrap and refrigerate until the batter is firm, at least 4 hours or up to overnight.

4. Preheat the vegetable oil in a deep fryer to 350°F. Set a wire rack over a paper-towel-lined baking sheet.

5. Unmold the chickpea batter onto a cutting board, removing both sheets of waxed paper. Cut it in half lengthwise, and then slice the halves crosswise into ½-inch-wide sticks. Fry the chickpea sticks, in two batches, until golden brown, 2 to 3 minutes. Using a slotted spoon, transfer the fries to the wire rack to drain. Sprinkle with salt and serve immediately.

Fried Pickles

Serve these up next to your favorite sandwich or put them out with drinks the next time folks come over for a real flavor explosion!

One 16-ounce jar sliced dill pickles
1 cup buttermilk (see Note, page 105)
2 tablespoons Louisiana hot sauce
½ cup all-purpose flour
½ cup cornmeal
1 tablespoon Creole Seasoning (page 29)
    or Emeril's Original Essence,
      plus more for dusting
Vegetable oil, for deep-frying

1. Drain the pickles in a colander, and then spread them on paper towels to drain completely.

2. Combine the buttermilk and hot sauce in a small mixing bowl. In a separate bowl, combine the flour, cornmeal, and Creole Seasoning.

3. Preheat the vegetable oil in a deep fryer to 350°F. Line a baking sheet with paper towels.

4. Working in batches, submerge the pickle slices in the buttermilk, and then dredge them in the flour mixture, tossing to coat evenly. Shake to remove any excess flour. Fry the pickles until they are golden brown and crisp, 2 to 4 minutes. Drain briefly on the paper towels and serve hot or warm.

Hushpuppies

For an unmistakable jalapeño flavor, be
sure to include the seeds. These puppies are
a must to serve up at your next fish fry.

Vegetable oil, for deep-frying

1 cup yellow cornmeal

1 cup all-purpose flour

1 tablespoon sugar

1½ teaspoons salt

½ teaspoon freshly ground black pepper

1 teaspoon baking powder

1 teaspoon baking soda

2 eggs, beaten

1 cup buttermilk (see Note, page 105)

1 large yellow onion, grated

½ cup finely chopped green onion, white and
    green parts (about 3 green onions)

2 jalapeños, minced

Kicked-Up Tartar Sauce (recipe follows), for
    serving (optional)

1. Preheat the vegetable oil in a deep fryer
to 375°F. Set a wire rack over a paper-towel-
lined baking sheet.

2. Combine the cornmeal, flour, sugar,
salt, pepper, baking powder, and baking
soda in a large mixing bowl. In a second
mixing bowl, whisk together the eggs,
buttermilk, grated onion, green onion, and
jalapeño. Add the wet ingredients to the dry
ingredients and whisk gently to combine.

3. Working with batches of 6 or 7, drop
heaping tablespoonfuls of the batter into
the hot oil and fry them, turning them
occasionally, until golden brown on all
sides and cooked through, 2 to 3 minutes.
Using a slotted spoon, transfer the cooked
hushpuppies to the prepared baking sheet.

4. Serve hot, with Kicked-Up Tartar Sauce if
desired.

Kicked-Up Tartar Sauce About 1½ cups

1 cup mayonnaise

¼ cup finely chopped cornichons or dill pickles,
    or drained dill pickle relish

2 tablespoons minced shallot

2 tablespoons minced green onion tops

1 tablespoon finely chopped drained nonpareil
    capers

1 tablespoon finely chopped fresh parsley leaves

2 teaspoons Creole mustard or other spicy
    whole-grain mustard

½ teaspoon Louisiana hot sauce

¼ teaspoon cayenne pepper

¼ teaspoon dried tarragon, crushed between
    your fingers

1. Combine all the ingredients in a small
bowl and stir well to blend. Refrigerate until
ready to serve.

2. The sauce, covered, will keep for up to
1 week in the refrigerator.

Fried Kicked-Up Jalapeño Poppers

Everyone loves poppers, and this bacon-y version will be a hit at your next party. They have a panko coating that makes them extra-crispy! When shopping for the peppers, try to select large jalapeños that are unwaxed and ungreased—any shiny coating will prevent the batter from adhering to the peppers.

16 to 20 large jalapeños
8 ounces cream cheese, at room temperature
½ cup grated Monterey Jack cheese
6 strips bacon, cooked crisp and crumbled
2 teaspoons kosher salt, plus more for
  sprinkling
½ cup plus 3 tablespoons all-purpose flour
½ cup whole milk
1 large egg, lightly beaten
1½ cups panko breadcrumbs
Vegetable oil, for deep-frying

1. Cut a lengthwise slit down one side of each jalapeño to create a pocket, leaving the stem intact. Using a paring knife or a small spoon, carefully scrape the inside to remove at least some of the seeds in order to make room for the filling.

2. Combine the cream cheese, Monterey Jack, bacon, and ½ teaspoon of the salt in a small bowl. Place the mixture in a resealable plastic food storage bag or a large piping bag. (If using a food storage bag, cut one corner of the bag to form a hole that's large enough to allow the bacon pieces to squeeze through.) Squeeze the mixture to the bottom of the bag, and then fill each pepper with as much of the cream cheese mixture as will fit. Press the slit edges of the pepper together to seal. The peppers can be prepared up to this point up to a day in advance and refrigerated, covered, until ready to fry.

3. In a small bowl, combine the ½ cup flour, milk, and egg. Place the remaining 3 tablespoons flour, the panko crumbs, and the remaining 1½ teaspoons salt in a shallow bowl or plate, and stir to combine.

4. Preheat the vegetable oil in a deep fryer to 375°F. Line a baking sheet with paper towels.

5. Working in batches, dip the stuffed jalapeños into the milk batter and then roll them in the panko mixture, pressing to coat. As they are breaded, gently place the jalapeños in the fryer and cook until golden brown, 3 to 4 minutes. Transfer the poppers to the prepared baking sheet to drain briefly. Then place them on a serving plate and sprinkle lightly with salt. Allow the poppers to cool slightly before serving.

Fried Eggplant with Confectioners' Sugar

Though it may sound odd to sprinkle confectioners' sugar on eggplant, you've just got to trust me on this one. This is a very traditional way to enjoy eggplant in New Orleans, and some of our grandest Creole restaurants have had this on the menu for nearly a century!

Vegetable oil, for deep-frying
2 medium eggplants, peeled and cut into
    ½-inch batons, 3 to 4 inches long
Salt
2 eggs
2 tablespoons granulated sugar
¼ cup plus 1 tablespoon all-purpose flour
Confectioners' sugar, for serving

1. Preheat the vegetable oil in a deep fryer to 350°F. Position a wire rack over a paper-towel-lined baking sheet.

2. Season the eggplant batons lightly with salt.

3. In a mixing bowl, whisk the eggs until frothy. Whisk in the granulated sugar and a pinch of salt. Then whisk in the flour; the mixture will resemble a light batter. Soak the eggplant batons in the batter briefly.

4. When you are ready to fry them, remove the eggplant batons from the batter one at a time, allowing the excess batter to drip off, and then gently lay the batons in the hot oil. Fry the eggplant for 2 to 3 minutes on each side, until golden brown. Remove from the oil with a slotted spoon, and drain on the wire rack.

5. Serve the eggplant immediately, sprinkled with confectioners' sugar.

Feta Fries

Every spring, in the Lakeview neighborhood of New Orleans, thousands flock to the Greek Fest. There you can dance until weary, toast your dance partner with ouzo, and enjoy spit-roasted lamb, spanakopita, Greek salads, moussaka, baklava sundaes, and something they call "Greek Fries." This is my version, in which crisp fries are sprinkled with Greek herbs, lemon zest, crushed red pepper, and a just-right amount of salty feta cheese.

4 large russet potatoes, peeled and cut into
    ½-inch-thick fries
Vegetable oil, for deep-frying
Kosher salt
3 teaspoons minced fresh oregano leaves
1 teaspoon minced fresh rosemary leaves
1 teaspoon minced fresh thyme leaves
1 teaspoon minced fresh marjoram leaves
Finely grated zest of 1 lemon
Crushed red pepper, to taste
4 ounces Greek feta or other salty feta cheese,
    crumbled

1. Place the cut fries in a large bowl of ice water and allow to chill for at least 2 hours or up to overnight.

2. Preheat the vegetable oil in a deep fryer to 325°F. Position a wire rack over a paper-towel-lined baking sheet.

3. Remove the fries from the ice water, transfer them to clean kitchen towels, and blot until thoroughly dry. Working in batches, fry the potatoes until they are tender but not colored, 2 to 3 minutes. Transfer them to the wire rack to drain and let them sit for at least 10 minutes.

4. Raise the fryer temperature to 375°F.

5. Working in batches, fry the fries a second time until crisp and golden brown, usually 2 to 3 minutes. Transfer them to the wire rack to drain briefly.

6. Sprinkle the fries lightly with salt, and then transfer them to a serving dish. Sprinkle with the minced herbs, lemon zest, crushed red pepper, and feta cheese.

Light and Crispy Fried Onion Rings

These crisp, feather-light onion rings soak up loads of flavor while marinating briefly in an intensely flavored buttermilk mixture. Although the amount of hot sauce might seem excessive, you've got to trust me here: it's just the right amount to impart a subtle yet tangy little kick.

3 cups buttermilk (see Note, page 105)
¾ cup Louisiana hot sauce, such as Crystal or Original Louisiana Hot Sauce
2 tablespoons Creole Seasoning (page 29) or Emeril's Original Essence
3 teaspoons cayenne pepper
2 large sweet onions, such as Vidalia, Maui, or Walla Walla, sliced crosswise into ½-inch-thick rings
Vegetable oil, for deep-frying
2 cups all-purpose flour
2 teaspoons baking powder
1 teaspoon kosher salt, plus more for seasoning

1. Combine the buttermilk, hot sauce, Creole Seasoning, and 2 teaspoons of the cayenne in a large mixing bowl. Separate the onion slices into individual rings (discard the small center portions or save them for another purpose). Add the onion rings to the buttermilk mixture and stir gently to coat. Refrigerate until chilled, 45 minutes to 1 hour.

2. Preheat the vegetable oil in a deep fryer to 375°F. Position a wire rack over a paper-towel-lined baking sheet.

3. In a medium bowl, combine the flour, baking powder, salt, and remaining 1 teaspoon cayenne.

4. Working in batches, remove the onion rings from the buttermilk mixture, allowing the excess to drip back into the bowl, and dredge them in the flour mixture. Remove the coated rings from the flour, shake to remove any excess, and place them on the wire rack. Repeat until you have coated all the onion rings.

5. Working in batches, fry the onion rings, turning them occasionally, until crisp and golden, about 3 minutes. Transfer them to the wire rack to drain briefly. Season lightly with salt and serve immediately.

Tostones with Mojo Sauce

Tostones (toas-TOH-nays) are twice-fried plantains, and if you've never experienced this Latin snack, you're in for a treat! Although tostones are most commonly made with green plantains, which are starchy and fibrous, if you use plantains that are slightly yellow, the flavor is a bit sweeter and the texture a bit softer. Either way, we love these with the intensely flavored Mojo Sauce, which in all honesty would be good on just about anything.

Vegetable oil, for deep-frying
3 large green or slightly yellow plantains
Kosher or sea salt, for sprinkling
Mojo Sauce (recipe follows), for serving

1. Heat the vegetable oil in a deep fryer to 350°F. Line a baking sheet with paper towels.

2. With a sharp knife, cut the ends from each plantain and score the skins lengthwise several times to help remove the skin. Peel the plaintains, and then cut them crosswise into ¾-inch-thick slices. In batches, deep-fry the plantain pieces until just golden, 2 to 3 minutes. Using tongs, transfer the pieces to the prepared baking sheet to drain.

3. Cut two pieces of parchment paper into 12-inch lengths. Place one piece on a flat work surface and place a few of the oil-blanched plantain slices on the parchment. Cover with the second sheet of parchment, and using the bottom of a heavy pot (such as a cast-iron skillet), press down firmly on the plantains to flatten them to about ¼-inch thickness. Repeat with the remaining slices.

4. Working in batches, fry the tostones a second time, until they are golden brown and crisp, 2 to 3 minutes. Then transfer them to the prepared baking sheet to drain briefly. Sprinkle with salt and serve hot or warm, with the Mojo Sauce for dipping.

Mojo Sauce About 1½ cups

¾ cup mild extra-virgin olive oil
½ cup chopped sweet onion
3 tablespoons minced garlic (6 to 8 cloves)
3 fresh green chiles, such as jalapeño or
   serrano, roasted (see page 19), peeled,
   stemmed, and seeded
½ cup loosely packed fresh cilantro leaves

3 tablespoons freshly squeezed lime juice,
   or more to taste
2 tablespoons freshly squeezed lemon juice,
   or more to taste
2 teaspoons sea salt
Honey or agave nectar, to taste
   (optional; see Notes)

In a small saucepan, heat the oil with the onion and garlic over medium heat until the oil bubbles around the edges and the sauce is fragrant, 3 to 4 minutes. Remove from the heat and allow to cool briefly. Then transfer the mixture to a blender or food processor and add the chiles, cilantro, lime juice, lemon juice, and salt. Process briefly to blend—the sauce may either be left slightly chunky or processed until smooth, as desired. Taste, and adjust the seasoning by adding honey, more lemon or lime juice, or more salt, all to taste.

NOTES: *If the plantains you use for your tostones are very green, you may want to add a bit of honey or agave nectar to the Mojo Sauce.*

The sauce may be used immediately or refrigerated in an airtight container until you are ready to use it, up to 1 week. If refrigerated, allow to come to room temperature before serving.

Mozzarella en Carozza with Puttanesca Dipping Sauce

Translated from the Italian, *mozzarella en carozza* means "mozzarella in clothes." In this instance, the clothes are the slices of bread that envelop slices of fresh mozzarella. The entire sandwich is dipped in an egg wash, coated in breadcrumbs, deep-fried, and served with a puttanesca sauce. The anchovy schmear on the inside of the bread really makes this dish come together, but those of you out there who shun this tiny salty fish can simply leave them out. You may need to add a little extra salt in that case.

8 ounces fresh mozzarella cheese, cut into
    ¼-inch-thick slices
12 slices white sandwich bread
1 tablespoon mashed canned anchovies
    (4 to 6 anchovy fillets)
2 tablespoons extra-virgin olive oil
1 tablespoon minced fresh parsley leaves
6 large eggs
2 teaspoons salt
2 cups coarse dry breadcrumbs, preferably
    homemade
Vegetable oil, for deep-frying
Puttanesca Dipping Sauce (recipe follows)

1. Divide the mozzarella slices evenly among 6 slices of the bread. In a small bowl, combine the anchovies, olive oil, and parsley. Spread a thin coating of the anchovy mixture onto the remaining 6 slices of bread. Put the anchovy-schmeared pieces of bread together with the mozzarella-topped bread so that the cheese and anchovy sides meet to form sandwiches. Trim the crusts from the bread to create neat, even edges. Cut the sandwiches in half on the diagonal to make triangles. (If you like, cut each triangle again in half so that each sandwich makes 4 smaller triangles. The smaller triangles are perfect for hors d'oeuvres.)

2. In a medium mixing bowl, whisk the eggs with the salt. Place the breadcrumbs in a separate bowl. Working with one at a time, dip the sandwiches in the egg wash to coat them, allow any excess to drip back into the bowl, and then place them in the breadcrumbs and turn to coat.

3. Preheat the vegetable oil in a deep fryer to 350°F. Position a wire rack over a paper-towel-lined baking sheet.

4. Working in batches, fry the sandwiches, turning them as necessary to promote even browning, until crisp and golden, 2 to 3 minutes. Transfer them to the wire rack to drain briefly. Serve with the Puttanesca Dipping Sauce.

Puttanesca Dipping Sauce About 3 cups

This sauce is also terrific tossed with pasta or used as a sauce for pizza.

2 tablespoons olive oil
½ cup finely chopped yellow onion
1 tablespoon minced garlic (2 to 3 cloves)
One 28-ounce can whole Italian plum tomatoes,
    with juices, pureed in a blender
½ cup pitted and finely chopped
    Kalamata olives
1 tablespoon tomato paste
1 tablespoon drained nonpareil capers
1 tablespoon minced canned anchovy fillets
    (4 to 6 fillets)
½ teaspoon crushed red pepper
Salt

1. In a medium saucepan, heat the olive oil over medium-high heat. Add the onion and sauté until it is soft and lightly caramelized, about 5 minutes. Add the garlic and cook until fragrant, 1 to 2 minutes. Add the pureed tomatoes and the olives, tomato paste, capers, anchovy, and crushed red pepper. Simmer until the sauce is thickened and slightly reduced, about 20 minutes.

2. Add salt to taste, cover, and set aside. Serve the sauce warm or at room temperature.

3. Any unused sauce can be refrigerated, covered, for up to 1 week.

Arancini

Arancini are balls of leftover risotto that are stuffed and then breaded and deep-fried. In Italy, when arancini are stuffed with cheese, they're sometimes called *suppli al telefono*, or "telephone cords"—referring to the way the cheese stretches as you pull them apart. Here we give you a basic risotto recipe and show you how to turn it into something spectacular for your next party. If you happen to already have leftover risotto at home, you can skip the risotto part and go straight to the stuffing.

Risotto

4 cups homemade chicken stock (see page 5) or packaged low-sodium chicken broth

4 tablespoons (½ stick) unsalted butter

1 medium yellow onion, finely chopped

1 cup Carnaroli or Arborio rice

3 cloves garlic, minced

½ cup dry white wine

½ cup finely grated Parmigiano-Reggiano cheese, plus extra for garnish

¼ cup heavy cream

1½ tablespoons chopped mixed fresh herbs, such as basil, thyme, parsley, or chives

1¼ teaspoons kosher salt

½ teaspoon freshly ground black pepper

Arancini

3 eggs

4 ounces fresh mozzarella cheese, cut into ½-inch cubes

2 ounces prosciutto or ham, finely chopped

1 cup all-purpose flour

1½ cups coarse dry breadcrumbs, preferably homemade, or panko

Vegetable oil, for deep-frying

Warmed marinara sauce, for dipping (optional)

1. To make the risotto, bring the stock to a simmer in a saucepan. Cover and set aside to keep hot.

2. In a heavy Dutch oven or large saucepan, melt the butter over medium-high heat. Add the onion and sauté until translucent, about 4 minutes. Add the rice and garlic and cook, stirring constantly, until rice is opaque and fragrant, 1 to 2 minutes. Add the wine and cook, stirring, until it has been absorbed. While continually stirring, begin adding the hot stock in ½-cup increments, allowing the liquid to become completely absorbed between additions. Cook until the rice is just tender and the risotto is creamy, usually about 20 minutes.

3. Add the grated Parmesan, heavy cream, herbs, salt, and pepper to the risotto, and stir to combine well. Transfer the risotto to a medium bowl or baking dish and allow it to cool completely. Then refrigerate until thoroughly chilled, at least 6 hours.

4. When you are ready to make the arancini, remove the chilled risotto from the refrigerator and stir in one of the eggs. Using a small scoop or a large spoon, divide the risotto into 3-tablespoon portions. Using

your hands, form the portions into rough ball shapes.

5. Press a hole into the center of each risotto ball, and stuff the center with a cube of the cheese and some of the chopped prosciutto. Press the opening closed and roll the ball between your hands until it is smooth. Set the stuffed rice balls aside.

6. Line a baking sheet with parchment paper. Place the flour, the remaining 2 eggs, and the breadcrumbs into three separate bowls. Using a fork, lightly beat the eggs. One by one, lightly dredge each risotto ball first in the flour, then in the beaten egg, and then in the breadcrumbs, so that each ball is completely coated. Place the coated arancini on the prepared baking sheet and refrigerate until you are ready to fry them.

7. When you're ready to fry the arancini, preheat vegetable oil in a deep fryer to 350°F. Position a wire rack over a paper-towel-lined baking sheet.

8. Fry the arancini in batches, about 6 at a time, turning them during cooking so that they are evenly browned, 5 to 6 minutes. As they are cooked, transfer them to the wire rack to drain briefly. Serve hot, with warm marinara sauce for dipping if desired.

Fried Polenta with Parsley-Tomato Drizzle

12 appetizer or 6 entrée servings

Polenta is a dish that can wear many hats. Not only can a simple bowl of creamy polenta sprinkled with cheese be fabulous on its own, but it also makes a delicious backdrop on which to serve a robust meat stew (see the photo on page 171). And when you take polenta that's left to cool and firm up and then fry it to form crisp little pillows of goodness, look out! Topped with an herb-packed olive oil, sweet tomatoes, and aged Asiago cheese, this dish makes an equally fantastic first course or vegetarian entrée.

Polenta

Olive oil, for greasing the pan
6½ cups water
1 tablespoon kosher salt
2 cups fine yellow cornmeal
½ cup heavy cream
2 ounces cream cheese or mascarpone cheese
¼ teaspoon finely ground white pepper
¾ cup instant flour, such as Wondra

Parsley-tomato drizzle

2 cups extra-virgin olive oil
1 cup loosely packed coarsely chopped fresh parsley leaves
4 teaspoons minced garlic (4 cloves)
4 teaspoons minced fresh rosemary leaves
1 tablespoon minced canned anchovies (4 to 6 fillets)
½ teaspoon crushed red pepper

8 ounces grape tomatoes, thinly sliced crosswise
Vegetable oil, for deep-frying

Garnish

1½ cups coarsely grated aged Asiago cheese
1 cup coarsely chopped walnuts
Sea salt or kosher salt

1. Generously coat a 9 x 12-inch rimmed baking sheet or baking pan with olive oil.

2. In a heavy large saucepan, bring the water and salt to a rolling boil. While whisking constantly, add the cornmeal in a steady stream until it is completely incorporated and no trace of lumps remains. When the polenta comes to a boil and thickens somewhat, partially cover the saucepan and reduce the heat to a steady simmer. Cook the polenta, stirring occasionally, until it is tender and very thick, 30 to 40 minutes. Then whisk in the cream, cream cheese, and white pepper.

3. Working quickly, turn the polenta out onto the oiled baking sheet and use an offset spatula or the back of a spoon to spread it out to an even thickness. Set aside and allow to cool. Then wrap the whole thing in plastic wrap and refrigerate it until the polenta is thoroughly chilled and very firm, at least several hours and up to 2 days in advance.

4. Shortly before you are ready to serve the polenta, make the parsley-tomato drizzle: In a medium bowl, combine the olive oil, parsley, garlic, rosemary, anchovies, crushed red pepper, and tomatoes. Stir to combine, and set aside at room temperature.

5. Preheat the vegetable oil in a deep fryer to 350°F. Line a baking sheet with paper towels.

6. Place the instant flour in a shallow bowl. Cut the polenta into 12 squares and dredge each square in the instant flour.

7. Working in batches, fry the coated polenta squares, making sure they don't touch one another and turning them to promote even browning, until they are golden brown and crispy, 8 to 10 minutes. Transfer them to the prepared baking sheet to drain briefly.

8. Serve the polenta squares with the parsley-tomato drizzle generously spooned over the top, and garnished with the Asiago, walnuts, and salt to taste.

Crabmeat Beignets

These crabmeat beignets are like a marriage of a crabcake and a fritter . . . light and airy but chock-full of jumbo lump crabmeat. The batter is a little wet, so handle with care when frying.

1 cup diced red bell pepper
    (1 small pepper, small dice)
1 jalapeño, stemmed, seeded,
    and cut into small dice
2 green onions, minced
1½ teaspoons salt
¼ teaspoon Worcestershire sauce
¼ teaspoon hot sauce
⅔ cup all-purpose flour
3 tablespoons cornmeal
½ teaspoon baking powder
⅛ teaspoon cayenne pepper
⅓ cup whole milk
2 eggs, lightly beaten
1 pound fresh jumbo lump crabmeat,
    picked over for shells and cartilage
Vegetable oil, for deep-frying
1 cup instant flour, such as Wondra
Tartar or rémoulade sauce, for serving

1. In a small bowl, combine the bell pepper, jalapeño, green onion, ¾ teaspoon of the salt, the Worcestershire sauce, and the hot sauce. Set aside.

2. In a separate bowl, combine the all-purpose flour, cornmeal, baking powder, and cayenne and mix well. Stir in the milk and eggs. Fold in the bell pepper mixture and the crabmeat. Let the mixture rest for 15 minutes.

3. Preheat the vegetable oil in a deep fryer to 350°F. Preheat the oven to 250°F. Position a wire rack over a paper-towel-lined baking sheet.

4. Combine the instant flour and the remaining ¾ teaspoon salt in a shallow dish or baking pan.

5. Using a small ice cream scoop or a measuring spoon and working in batches, drop 2 rounded tablespoonfuls of the beignet batter into the instant flour and toss to coat. Gently drop the beignets into the fryer. Do not overcrowd the fryer. Cook the beignets until golden brown, about 2 minutes per side. Drain the beignets on the wire rack. Repeat with the remaining beignet batter, keeping the drained cooked beignets warm in the oven.

6. Serve the beignets immediately, with tartar sauce or rémoulade sauce.

Shrimp Tempura

I use skewers here to give the shrimp the characteristic sushi house look: long and straight. The skewers aren't necessary, though. What's most important is that your tempura batter is very cold. Make sure that the seltzer is cold when making the batter, and after your first batch of shrimp you may even want to set the batter over an ice bath as you proceed.

2 pounds large shrimp, peeled, deveined,
    last tail segment left intact
Vegetable oil, for deep frying
½ cup ponzu sauce
2 tablespoons dark Asian sesame oil
¼ cup thinly sliced green onion
    (about 2 green onions)
½ cup water
Sriracha sauce, to taste
1 cup rice flour
½ cup cornstarch
¾ teaspoon salt
½ teaspoon freshly ground black pepper
One 12-ounce can seltzer water,
    well chilled
1 cup all-purpose flour

1. At least 1 hour before serving, insert a 6-inch skewer from the tail to the head of each shrimp so that it is straight. Cover and refrigerate.

2. Preheat the vegetable oil in a deep fryer to 375°F. Set a wire rack over a paper-towel-lined baking sheet.

3. Combine the ponzu sauce with the sesame oil, green onion, and water in a small bowl. Add a few drops of Sriracha sauce and set aside until ready to serve.

4. Remove the shrimp from the refrigerator. If it is easier for you, remove and discard the skewers. But if you choose, you can also leave them in and remove them after frying.

5. Make the tempura batter by combining the rice flour with the cornstarch, salt, and pepper in a shallow container. Whisk in the cold seltzer.

6. Place the all-purpose flour in a shallow dish.

7. Working in batches of 3 or 4, hold a shrimp by the tail (or the tail end of the skewer), and dredge it in the all-purpose flour, dip it in the batter, and add it to the fryer. Fry the shrimp until golden, about 3 minutes. Set the cooked shrimp on the wire rack to drain. You will need to whisk the tempura batter thoroughly before dredging each batch of shrimp.

8. Serve the shrimp immediately, with the ponzu sauce alongside.

Classic Crab Rangoons

Crab rangoons are on almost every menu in Chinese restaurants across the country, but it is more than likely an American invention. These deep-fried creamy crab-and-cheese pillows are a sure-fire hit for your next party. Serve them with the sauce below, or with a hot mustard sauce, plum sauce, or sweet and sour chili sauce, and watch them disappear as quickly as you make them.

1 pound Neufchâtel cheese, at room temperature
¼ cup minced green onion (about 2 green onions)
1 teaspoon Worcestershire sauce
1 teaspoon soy sauce
½ teaspoon sambal oelek sauce, chili garlic sauce, or Sriracha sauce
3 strips bacon, cooked crisp and crumbled
1 pound fresh claw crabmeat
½ teaspoon kosher salt
1 package dumpling wrappers
Vegetable oil, for deep-frying
Chili Garlic Dipping Sauce (recipe follows), for serving

1. In a medium bowl, combine the cheese, green onion, Worcestershire sauce, soy sauce, and sambal oelek sauce, and mix well. Fold in the bacon and crabmeat, and season with the salt (or to taste).

2. Working with 4 at a time, place the dumpling wrappers on a work surface. Spoon about 2 tablespoons of the crabmeat mixture onto the center of each wrapper and wet the edges. Fold two opposite corners up to meet over the filling, forming a triangle shape, and press to seal the edges (try to squeeze out any air that gets in). Now fold the two bottom points of the triangle together and press to seal, moistening with a bit of water. Set the dumplings on a baking sheet and cover them with a damp cloth to prevent them from drying out while you assemble the remaining rangoons.

3. Preheat the vegetable oil in a deep fryer to 375°F. Preheat the oven to 250°F. Position a wire rack over a paper-towel-lined baking sheet.

4. Working in batches, fry the crab rangoons until they are golden brown, about 3 minutes. As they are cooked, transfer them to the wire rack to drain briefly. Once the rack is full, transfer the crab rangoons to a baking sheet in the oven to keep warm.

5. Serve with the Chili Garlic Dipping Sauce.

Chili Garlic Dipping Sauce About ¾ cup

¼ cup chili garlic sauce

¼ cup honey

2 tablespoons rice vinegar

2 teaspoons dark Asian sesame oil

2 teaspoons soy sauce

Combine all the ingredients in a small bowl and whisk well.

NOTE: *The sauce can be scaled up proportionally if desired.*

Fried Calamari with Lemon Aïoli and Olive Salad

I've served fried calamari with olive salad at my restaurants for years, and guests never seem to tire of it. Here I've amped it up a bit with a simple lemon aïoli.

1½ pounds calamari (bodies and tentacles), cleaned, bodies cut into ¼-inch-wide rings
½ cup buttermilk (see Note, page 105)
2 tablespoons Creole Seasoning (page 29) or Emeril's Original Essence
Vegetable oil, for deep-frying
3 cups all-purpose flour
Salt, to taste
Lemon Aïoli (recipe follows)
Olive Salad (recipe follows)

1. Combine the calamari, buttermilk, and Creole Seasoning in a bowl. Cover and refrigerate for at least 30 minutes and up to 4 hours.

2. Preheat the vegetable oil in a deep fryer to 375°F. Line a baking sheet with paper towels or a kitchen towel.

3. Add the flour to a large bowl. Set a straining basket over another mixing bowl. Dredge one-quarter of the calamari in the flour, then add it to the straining basket and shake gently to remove any excess flour. Transfer the calamari to the fryer and cook until golden, about 1 minute.

4. Transfer the fried calamari to the prepared baking sheet to drain, and season with salt. Repeat with the remaining calamari.

5. Serve immediately, with the Lemon Aïoli and Olive Salad.

Lemon Aïoli 1¼ cups

1 large egg yolk
Grated zest of 1 lemon
2 tablespoons freshly squeezed lemon juice
1 tablespoon minced garlic (2 to 3 cloves)
½ teaspoon salt
Pinch of freshly ground black pepper
1 cup vegetable oil

In a small bowl, whisk the egg yolk, lemon zest, lemon juice, garlic, salt, and pepper together. While whisking vigorously, add the oil in a thin, steady stream until it is completely incorporated and emulsified. Serve immediately, or cover and refrigerate for up to 2 days.

Olive Salad 2 cups

1 cup black olives, such as Kalamata,
    pitted and sliced
1 cup pimento-stuffed green olives, such as
    Spanish olives, sliced
2 tablespoons minced shallot
2 tablespoons minced celery
2 tablespoons chopped fresh parsley leaves

2 teaspoons minced garlic
2 tablespoons balsamic vinegar
¼ cup extra-virgin olive oil

Combine all the ingredients in a small bowl. Serve immediately, or cover and refrigerate for up to 1 week.

Crawfish Hand Pies

Natchitoches meat pies and crawfish pies are two favorites at the New Orleans Jazz & Heritage Festival. My version of crawfish pie here is made with a creamy crawfish and rice filling that is wrapped in flaky pie dough and then deep-fried. You can make the pies any size you like, but I like to make them on the smaller side and serve them up as appetizers.

6 tablespoons (¾ stick) unsalted butter
½ cup chopped yellow onion (½ small onion)
¼ cup chopped green bell pepper
   (¼ bell pepper)
¼ cup chopped celery (½ rib)
1 teaspoon chopped garlic (1 large clove)
2 teaspoons Worcestershire sauce
1 teaspoon salt, plus more for seasoning
¾ teaspoon cayenne pepper
¼ cup all-purpose flour, plus more for dusting
1¼ cups whole milk
1 pound cooked and peeled crawfish tails
¾ cup steamed long-grain white rice
¼ cup chopped green onion
   (about 2 green onions)
¼ cup chopped fresh parsley leaves
Pie Dough (recipe follows), at room temperature
Vegetable oil, for deep-frying

1. Heat the butter in a medium sauté pan over medium-high heat. Once the butter starts to bubble, add the onion, bell pepper, celery, garlic, Worcestershire sauce, salt, and cayenne. Cook, stirring, until the vegetables are tender, about 5 minutes. Add the flour and cook, stirring, until the mixture is golden brown, about 4 minutes. Add the milk and continue stirring until the mixture becomes smooth and thick, 4 to 5 minutes. Add the crawfish tails and cook, stirring, for 2 to 3 minutes. Remove from the heat and add the cooked rice, green onion, and parsley. Check the seasoning and adjust as necessary. Set aside until cooled to room temperature.

2. Form the pie dough into a ball and cut it into 36 equal pieces, about 2 tablespoons each (divide the dough in thirds, and then each third again in thirds, and each of those sections into quarters). Dust each piece with a little flour and roll it out to form a 3½-inch round.

3. Place 1 tablespoonful of the crawfish mixture slightly off-center on each round, and fold the dough over so that the edges meet, forming a half-moon. Using the tines of a fork, crimp the edges to seal them.

4. Preheat the vegetable oil in a deep fryer to 350°F. Position a wire rack over a baking sheet lined with paper towels.

5. Working in batches so as to not overcrowd the fryer, place the crawfish pies in the hot oil and fry until golden brown, about 3 minutes. Transfer the pies to the wire rack to drain briefly, season lightly with salt, and serve immediately.

Pie Dough   Enough dough for 36 hand pies or 2 single-crust 9-inch pies

3 cups all-purpose flour
¾ teaspoon baking powder
¼ teaspoon salt
6 tablespoons solid vegetable shortening or lard
1 egg, beaten
¾ cup whole milk

1. Sift the flour, baking powder, and salt together into a mixing bowl. Using a fork or a pastry blender, cut the shortening into the flour mixture until it resembles coarse crumbs. In a small bowl, beat the egg and milk together. Work the egg mixture into the dry ingredients until you achieve a thick but workable dough.

2. At this point the dough can be formed into a ball, tightly wrapped, and refrigerated overnight or frozen for up to 1 month.

3. When you are ready to use the dough, allow it to come to room temperature.

Fried Fish Tacos with Corn and Tomato Salsa

Fish tacos are always a hit—whether served from taco trucks, roadside shacks, your neighborhood Mexican restaurant, or the comfort of your own home. Crispy battered fish make the best tacos—look for the freshest fish you can find. A flaky whitefish such as grouper, cod, haddock, or flounder works best.

Vegetable oil, for deep-frying
2 pounds skinless firm whitefish fillets,
    such as flounder or grouper, cut into
    tranches about ½-inch thick (see Note)
1¼ teaspoons kosher salt
¾ cup all-purpose flour
¾ cup cornmeal
⅓ cup instant flour, such as Wondra
1½ teaspoons ancho chile powder
1 teaspoon chili powder
½ teaspoon cayenne pepper
2 eggs, beaten
¼ cup buttermilk (see Note, page 105)
Corn and Tomato Salsa (recipe follows)
Serrano Crema (recipe follows)
Eight 8-inch flour or corn tortillas, warmed
    according to package directions
Avocado slices, for serving
Lime wedges, for serving

1. Preheat the vegetable oil in a deep fryer to 375°F. Line a baking sheet with paper towels.

2. Season the fish fillets with 1 teaspoon of the salt, and set aside.

3. In a small mixing bowl, combine the all-purpose flour, cornmeal, instant flour, ancho chile powder, chili powder, cayenne, and the remaining ¼ teaspoon salt and mix well.

4. In a small bowl, combine the eggs and buttermilk and whisk well.

5. Prepare a dredging station by setting up three shallow dishes or pans. Divide half the flour mixture between two of the dishes and pour the egg mixture into the third dish. Working in batches, dredge the fish in the flour mixture, then in the egg mixture, and then in flour mixture. Drop the fish into the fryer and fry for 3 minutes, or until the coating is golden brown and the fish is tender. Take care not to overcook the fish. As the fish pieces are done, transfer them to the prepared baking sheet to drain.

6. Divide the fried fish, Corn and Tomato Salsa, Serrano Crema, and avocado slices among the warm tortillas. Serve with the lime wedges alongside.

NOTE: Tranche *is a French culinary term used to describe a cut of fish, meat, or poultry. In general, a* tranche *is a thin cut that is made across a fillet to provide more surface area.*

Corn and Tomato Salsa 1 quart

2 ears fresh sweet corn, kernels cut from the cob
1 pound heirloom tomatoes, diced
6 jalapeños, stemmed, seeded, and finely diced
½ red onion, finely diced
½ orange bell pepper, stemmed, seeded, and finely diced
Freshly squeezed juice of 1 lime
1 teaspoon chili powder
½ teaspoon ancho chile powder
¼ teaspoon cayenne pepper
⅛ teaspoon ground cumin
½ cup grapeseed oil
Salt, to taste

1. In a large mixing bowl, combine all the ingredients and mix well. Let stand at room temperature for 1 hour before serving.

2. The salsa will keep, covered, in the refrigerator for up to 1 week. Allow it to come to room temperature before serving.

Serrano Crema About 1 cup

½ cup sour cream
6 serrano chiles, stemmed, seeded, and minced
2 tablespoons chopped fresh cilantro leaves, plus whole leaves for garnish
1 tablespoon freshly squeezed lime juice
¼ teaspoon sea salt
¼ teaspoon finely ground white pepper

1. Combine the sour cream, serranos, chopped cilantro, lime juice, salt, and white pepper in a blender and blend until smooth. Set aside until ready to serve.

2. The serrano crema can be made in advance and kept, covered, in the refrigerator for up to 2 days.

Southeast Asian Egg Rolls

The Vietnamese version of egg rolls is slightly different from its Chinese cousin. Rather than being stuffed with meat and cabbage, they're filled with a combination of pork, shrimp, and cellophane noodles. They're traditionally made with rice paper wrappers, which gives them a light, crispy skin. The rice paper wrappers can be a little difficult to work with because they have a tendency to bubble up while frying, but they're well worth the effort. If you are unable to find rice paper wrappers, you can use the egg roll or spring roll wrappers sold in the supermarket, but note that the texture will be completely different.

2 ounces cellophane noodles

1 pound medium shrimp, peeled, deveined, and finely chopped

8 ounces ground pork

½ medium yellow onion, minced

2 cloves garlic, minced

¼ cup finely chopped carrot

¼ cup finely chopped red bell pepper

¼ cup dried cloud ear mushrooms, rehydrated and chopped

¼ cup minced green onion (about 2 green onions)

¼ cup Vietnamese fish sauce

1½ teaspoons chili garlic sauce

1 package small (6-inch) round rice paper wrappers (*banh trang*; see Note)

Vegetable oil, for deep-frying

For serving

Red-leaf lettuce leaves

Fresh mint sprigs

Fresh cilantro or culantro sprigs

Fresh Thai basil sprigs

1 cup Thai-Style Sweet Chili Sauce (recipe follows)

1. Soak the cellophane noodles in a bowl of hot water for 20 minutes. Then drain and cut them into bite-size pieces.

2. In a medium bowl combine the shrimp, pork, onion, garlic, carrot, bell pepper, mushrooms, and green onion and mix well. Add the cellophane noodles, fish sauce, and chili garlic sauce and mix well. Set aside. The filling can be made up to 1 day ahead and kept, covered, in the refrigerator.

3. Fill a wide, shallow bowl with 2 inches of warm water, and place a damp paper towel or kitchen towel on your work surface.

4. Immerse a rice paper wrapper in the warm water and soak it very briefly (just a few seconds—it will continue to soften as you fill it); then lay the wrapper on the damp towel. Place a tablespoon of the filling onto the bottom quarter of the rice paper and press it into a 2-inch-long line. Roll the bottom edge of the rice paper over the filling and then fold both sides inward, and continue tightly rolling the wrapper up like a burrito. Place the finished roll, seam side

down, on a platter and cover it lightly with a damp cloth. Repeat the process with the remaining filling and wrappers.

5. Preheat the vegetable oil in a deep fryer to 350°F. Line a baking sheet with paper towels.

6. Working in batches, fry the rolls, making sure that they do not touch one another while frying. The rolls will begin to bubble and hiss and the wrappers will begin to change texture. Cook the rolls, turning them as necessary for even cooking, until golden brown, 7 to 10 minutes. As they are cooked, transfer the rolls to the prepared baking sheet.

7. Serve the rolls with the lettuce leaves, herbs, and Thai-Style Sweet Chili Sauce.

NOTE: Banh trang *is the Vietnamese name for rice paper wrappers. You may also see the French name,* gallettes de riz, *on the package.*

Thai-Style Sweet Chili Sauce 2 cups

1½ cups sugar

½ cup water

½ cup roughly chopped fresh cilantro leaves

2 ounces red jalapeños, stemmed, seeded, and coarsely chopped

2 ounces fresh red Thai bird chiles, stemmed, seeded, and coarsely chopped

¼ cup minced garlic (8 to 10 cloves)

2 tablespoons Vietnamese fish sauce

1. In a small saucepan, combine the sugar and water, stirring until the sugar has dissolved. Bring to a boil over medium-high heat, and then reduce the heat to a simmer. Let simmer for 5 minutes.

2. Remove the pan from the heat, add the cilantro, and let the cilantro steep in the syrup for 15 minutes. Then strain the syrup, discarding the solids. Set aside and let cool completely.

3. Place the chiles, garlic, and fish sauce in the bowl of a mini chopper or mini processor and pulse to a coarse texture. Add the chile mixture to the cilantro syrup and bring to a simmer. Simmer for 8 to 10 minutes, until the mixture has reduced by half. The sauce should be slightly thick and will continue to thicken as it sits.

4. Use immediately, or transfer to a jar and refrigerate. The sauce can be kept for up to 2 weeks in the refrigerator.

Smoked Trout Croquettes

This is a riff on salt cod fritters, and I think it's every bit as good. Salt cod can be difficult to find and must be soaked for several days in advance. Smoked trout or smoked whitefish, on the other hand, is readily accessible and requires no advance preparation. The key to this recipe is to use the baked potato as soon as it's cool enough to handle so that the potato is light and fluffy rather than starchy. It's a breeze after that.

One 1-pound baking potato, baked
8 ounces smoked trout or smoked whitefish, skinned and flaked
2 cloves garlic, minced
⅓ cup heavy cream
1 tablespoon chopped fresh parsley leaves
1 tablespoon chopped fresh chives
Salt, to taste
Freshly ground black pepper, to taste
2 eggs, separated
1 cup instant flour, such as Wondra
Vegetable oil, for deep-frying
Spanish Pimentón Aïoli (recipe follows), for serving

1. Scrape out the pulp of the baked potato into a mixing bowl and, using a masher, mash until smooth. Add the fish, garlic, heavy cream, parsley, chives, salt, pepper, and egg yolks. Mix well.

2. In a separate medium bowl, beat the egg whites until soft peaks form. Fold the egg whites into the fish-and-potato mixture.

3. Using a 3-tablespoon scoop, form the mixture into balls about the size of golf balls.

4. Place the instant flour in a shallow dish, and dredge the croquettes in the flour.

5. Preheat the vegetable oil in a deep fryer to 350°F. Set a wire rack over a paper-towel-lined baking sheet.

6. Fry the croquettes, in batches, until golden brown, about 3 minutes. As they are cooked, transfer them to the wire rack to drain. Season the croquettes with salt and pepper, and serve them on a platter with the aïoli alongside.

Spanish Pimentón Aïoli 1 cup

1 cup mayonnaise
1 tablespoon freshly squeezed lemon juice
1 clove garlic, minced

1 tablespoon pimentón dulce (sweet Spanish smoked paprika)
Pinch of salt

In a small mixing bowl, combine all the ingredients and mix well. Place in a resealable container and refrigerate for at least 1 hour. The aïoli will keep for up to 1 week.

Smokin' Chipotle Chicken Wings

This smoky take on traditional hot wings is sure to be a hit at your next football party!

4 pounds chicken wings, rinsed and patted dry

1½ cups all-purpose flour

1½ teaspoons salt

1 teaspoon freshly ground black pepper

8 ounces (2 sticks) unsalted butter, melted

5 chipotle chiles in adobo sauce, plus 2 tablespoons adobo sauce

3 tablespoons Louisiana hot sauce, such as Crystal or Original Louisiana Hot Sauce

1 tablespoon freshly squeezed lime juice

2 cloves garlic

1 teaspoon kosher salt

Vegetable oil, for deep-frying

1. Separate the chicken wings into drumettes and wingettes, discarding the wing tips (or save those for stock). Place the chicken wing pieces in a large resealable plastic food storage bag and add the flour, salt, and pepper. Shake the bag until the wings are well coated, and then transfer the wings and the remaining flour to a large baking sheet. Allow the chicken to sit for about 1 hour, tossing the wings occasionally in the extra flour on the baking sheet.

2. Combine the melted butter, chipotle chiles, adobo sauce, hot sauce, and lime juice in a blender. On a cutting board, use the side of a chef's knife to mash the garlic with the kosher salt to form a paste. Add the garlic paste to the blender, and process until the chipotle butter sauce is very smooth. Transfer the sauce to a small saucepan and cover to keep it warm until you are ready to serve the chicken.

3. Preheat the vegetable oil in a deep fryer to 350°F. Position a wire rack over a paper-towel-lined baking sheet.

4. Working in batches, shake the wings to remove any excess flour, and fry them until golden brown and crispy, 12 to 14 minutes. As they are cooked, transfer the wings to the wire rack to drain briefly, and then put them in a heat-proof mixing bowl and drizzle with some of the chipotle butter sauce. Toss until the wings are thoroughly coated. Any sauce left in the saucepan can be served with the wings for dipping.

Pork Boulettes with Creole Mustard Dipping Sauce

About 48 boulettes

In southeast Louisiana, folks take *boudin,* our beloved pork and rice sausage, remove it from its casing, and form it into balls that are then breaded and deep-fried. People go crazy for boudin balls, as they're known, and they are offered at many festivals and restaurants throughout the state. The word *boulette* is French for "little ball," and this recipe is based on boudin balls with one exception: boudin contains a bit of liver, which real boudin lovers love, but I've omitted it here for those who don't. The Creole mustard sauce is the perfect complement to these rich, meaty treats.

Pork boulettes

1 pound ground pork
4 teaspoons Creole Seasoning (page 29) or Emeril's Original Essence
4 tablespoons (½ stick) unsalted butter
1¼ cups all-purpose flour
1 medium yellow onion, chopped
⅓ cup chopped red bell pepper
3 cloves garlic, minced
1 tablespoon plus 1¾ teaspoons kosher salt
¼ teaspoon freshly ground black pepper
¼ teaspoon cayenne pepper
2 cups water
2 cups steamed medium- or long-grain white rice
½ bunch green onions, chopped
2 tablespoons minced fresh parsley leaves
2¼ cups coarse dry breadcrumbs, preferably homemade
2 large eggs
¼ cup milk
Vegetable oil, for deep-frying

Creole mustard dipping sauce

1 cup mayonnaise
5 tablespoons Creole mustard
2 cloves garlic, minced
¼ teaspoon cayenne pepper

1. In a large skillet over medium heat, combine the pork and Creole Seasoning and cook, stirring, until browned, about 5 minutes. Remove from the heat and transfer the meat to a sieve placed over a bowl to drain.

2. In the same skillet, melt the butter over medium heat. Add ¼ cup of the flour and cook, stirring constantly with a heatproof rubber spatula so that it does not scorch, until a dark brown roux is formed, about 5 minutes.

3. Add the onion and bell pepper to the roux, and cook, stirring, until the vegetables are soft, 3 minutes. Add the garlic and cook, stirring, for 30 seconds. Add the drained cooked pork and cook for

1 minute. Add ¾ teaspoon of the salt, the black pepper, cayenne, and water. Bring to a boil. Then reduce the heat and simmer, stirring occasionally, until thickened, about 20 minutes. Add the cooked rice, green onions, parsley, and ¼ cup of the breadcrumbs and cook, stirring, for 2 minutes.

4. Remove the skillet from the heat and spread the meat mixture on a baking sheet or platter. Set aside until it is cool enough to handle. (The mixture can be wrapped and refrigerated at this point until ready to proceed, up to several days in advance.)

5. In a shallow bowl, season the remaining 1 cup flour with 1 tablespoon of the remaining salt. In another shallow bowl, place the remaining 2 cups breadcrumbs. In a third shallow bowl, whisk the eggs together with the milk and the remaining 1 teaspoon salt.

6. With damp hands, shape the pork-and-rice mixture into balls the size of unshelled walnuts, about 2 tablespoons each. Dredge the pork balls in the flour, and then dip them in the egg wash, letting the excess drip off. Finally, dredge the balls in the breadcrumbs, turning to coat them evenly. Transfer the boulettes to a parchment-lined baking sheet and refrigerate for at least 30 minutes or up to overnight.

7. Preheat the vegetable oil in a deep fryer to 350°F. Line a baking sheet with paper towels.

8. Using a slotted spoon and working in batches, slide the boulettes gently into the oil and fry until golden, 3 to 4 minutes. Remove from the oil and drain briefly on the prepared baking sheet. Let them cool briefly before serving.

9. While the boulettes cool, make the Creole mustard dipping sauce: In a small bowl, stir together the mayonnaise, Creole mustard, garlic, and cayenne.

10. Serve the boulettes hot or warm, with the mustard dipping sauce alongside.

Natchitoches Meat Pies

Natchitoches (pronounced Nack-a-tish) is a town in Cajun country and is the oldest permanent settlement of the Louisiana Purchase. And though they are a regional dish featuring the area's Native American and Spanish heritage, these meat pies are enjoyed at festival after festival all throughout Louisiana all year long.

Meat pie filling

1 teaspoon vegetable oil
1 pound ground beef
8 ounces ground pork
1 medium yellow onion, chopped
2 green onions, chopped
½ medium bell pepper, chopped
2 ribs celery, chopped
1½ teaspoons salt
½ teaspoon freshly ground black pepper
¼ teaspoon cayenne pepper
2 tablespoons chopped garlic (4 to 6 cloves)
1 tablespoon all-purpose flour
1 cup homemade beef stock (see page 6) or packaged low-sodium beef broth
1 tablespoon Crystal hot sauce or your favorite hot sauce

Dough

3 cups all-purpose flour, plus more for dusting
1½ teaspoons salt
¾ teaspoon baking powder
6 tablespoons solid vegetable shortening
1 egg
¾ cup whole milk
Vegetable oil, for deep-frying

1. To make the filling, heat a large skillet over medium-high heat and add the 1 teaspoon vegetable oil. When the oil is hot, add the beef and pork and cook until browned, stirring as needed, about 5 minutes. Add the onion, green onion, bell pepper, celery, salt, black pepper, and cayenne and continue to cook, stirring as needed, until the vegetables are soft, about 8 minutes. Add the garlic and cook for 2 minutes. Stir in the flour and stock, bring the mixture to a simmer, and continue cooking until it has thickened slightly, about 1 minute. Remove from the heat, stir in the hot sauce, and allow the filling to cool completely. The filling can be made up to 2 days in advance and kept, covered, in the refrigerator.

2. To make the dough, sift the flour, salt, and baking powder together into a medium bowl. Using a fork or pastry blender, cut the shortening into the flour mixture until it resembles coarse crumbs. In a small mixing bowl, beat the egg and milk together. Add the egg mixture to the flour mixture and stir until you have a thick but workable dough. Form the dough into a ball and flatten it into a disk. You can use it immediately or wrap it tightly in plastic wrap and refrigerate it for up to 1 day.

3. Preheat the vegetable oil in a deep fryer to 375°F. Set a wire rack over a paper-towel-lined baking sheet.

4. Cut the dough into 24 equal pieces. On a work surface that's lightly dusted with flour, roll each piece out to form a 5½- to 6-inch round. Place 2 tablespoons of the meat mixture slightly off-center on a round of dough. Fold the dough over to make the edges meet, and crimp the edges with the tines of a fork to seal them.

5. Working in batches, fry the meat pies until they are golden brown on both sides, about 3 minutes. Transfer the pies to the wire rack to drain. Serve hot.

Old-Fashioned Cake Doughnuts

You're probably thinking that it's way too hard to make really good doughnuts at home, but in fact you can make incredibly delicious doughnuts in less time than it would take to drive to the doughnut shop! The kids will love to decorate them with their favorite sprinkles after dipping them in the chocolate glaze.

2 large eggs, beaten
1 cup buttermilk (see Note, page 105)
¼ cup crème fraîche
1 cup sugar
1½ teaspoons vanilla extract
1 teaspoon grated lemon zest
4 cups unbleached all-purpose flour,
    plus more for dusting
½ cup cake flour
2 teaspoons baking powder
½ teaspoon baking soda
¼ teaspoon freshly grated nutmeg
3 tablespoons unsalted butter, melted
Vegetable oil, for deep-frying
Chocolate Glaze (recipe follows), warm
White Chocolate Glaze (recipe follows),
    warm
Sprinkles (optional)

1. In a small mixing bowl, combine the eggs, buttermilk, crème fraîche, sugar, vanilla, and lemon zest.

2. In a medium bowl, combine the all-purpose flour, cake flour, baking powder, baking soda, and nutmeg. Combine the wet ingredients with the dry ingredients, and whisk in the melted butter. The dough will be fairly sticky.

3. Turn the dough out onto a floured surface, and sprinkle it with a little flour. Knead the dough 4 or 5 times or until it begins to come together. Using a well-floured rolling pin, roll the dough out until it is ½ inch thick.

4. Using a doughnut cutter dusted with flour, cut out the doughnuts. Save the holes to fry with the doughnuts. Any extra dough can be rerolled and cut.

5. Preheat the vegetable oil in a deep fryer to 375°F. Position a wire rack over a paper-towel-lined baking sheet.

6. Working in batches, fry the doughnuts for 1½ minutes per side, or until golden brown. The doughnuts will sink initially but should pop right up. As they are done, transfer the doughnuts to the wire rack to drain and cool.

7. Once the doughnuts are cool, dip one side of half the doughnuts in the Chocolate Glaze and the other doughnuts in the White Chocolate Glaze. Decorate the doughnuts with colored sprinkles if you like.

Chocolate Glaze 1½ cups

⅓ cup unsalted butter
4 ounces good-quality semisweet chocolate
    (see Note)
2 cups confectioners' sugar
¼ cup warm water

Heat the butter and chocolate together in a medium saucepan over low heat until melted. Remove the pan from the heat and whisk in the confectioners' sugar until smooth. Gradually stir in the warm water until the mixture reaches the desired consistency. The glaze will harden as it sits, but it can be reheated carefully in a double boiler.

White Chocolate Glaze 1½ cups

⅓ cup unsalted butter
4 ounces good-quality white chocolate
    (see Note)
2 cups confectioners' sugar
¼ cup warm water

Heat the butter and chocolate together in a medium saucepan over low heat until melted. Remove the pan from the heat, and whisk in the confectioners' sugar until smooth. Gradually stir in the warm water until the mixture reaches the desired consistency. The glaze will harden as it sits, but it can be reheated carefully in a double boiler.

NOTE: *We used Green & Black's white and Ghirardelli semisweet chocolate bars for these glazes with great success.*

Cinnamon-Crusted Fried Peach Pies

This is the perfect indulgence to make in the summer, when ripe peaches are found at farm stands and farmers' markets. Although you could simplify this by using store-bought pie dough, I think that the tender, flaky cinnamon–cream cheese pastry here really makes these pies something special. Don't forget to dust them with sugar before serving!

Crust

2 cups all-purpose flour, plus more for dusting

3 tablespoons sugar, plus more for sprinkling

1¼ teaspoons ground cinnamon

½ teaspoon salt

¼ cup cream cheese, diced and chilled

9 tablespoons solid vegetable shortening, chilled, plus more for frying

4 to 6 tablespoons ice water

Peach filling

1 cup sugar

4 cups fresh (or frozen and thawed) peeled peach slices

4 whole cloves

¼ teaspoon freshly grated nutmeg

2 tablespoons freshly squeezed lemon juice

2 tablespoons water

3 tablespoons potato starch or cornstarch

Vegetable oil, for deep-frying

Vanilla bean ice cream or whipped cream, for serving (optional)

1. To make the crust, sift the flour, sugar, cinnamon, and salt into a large mixing bowl. Add the chilled cream cheese and shortening, and working with your hands or a fork, mix until the mixture resembles coarse meal. Add the ice water, 1 tablespoon at a time, and mix gently until the dough begins to stick together. Form the dough into a round disk, cover it with plastic wrap, and refrigerate it for at least 1 hour and up to overnight.

2. To make the peach filling, combine the sugar, peach slices, cloves, and nutmeg in a large saucepan over medium heat. Stir to combine. Bring the mixture to a boil. Then turn down the heat and allow the mixture to simmer until the peaches have softened, usually 10 to 15 minutes. Using a slotted spoon, remove the peaches from the saucepan and place them in a small bowl.

3. In another small bowl, combine the lemon juice, water, and potato starch. Whisk the starch mixture into the peach juices in the saucepan, stirring until combined. Bring the mixture to a boil and cook for 1 minute, stirring constantly to keep it from sticking; the mixture will be very thick. Transfer the thickened mixture to a clean bowl and remove the cloves. Gently fold in the softened peach slices. Refrigerate until thoroughly chilled, 3 to 4

hours. (The filling is best if used the day it is made, as the peaches tend to weep if left to sit overnight.)

4. Remove the dough from the refrigerator and divide it into 8 equal portions. On a lightly floured surface, roll out each piece of dough to form a thin round about 6 inches in diameter. Place ¼ cup of the chilled peach filling slightly off center of each dough round. Fold the dough over, making a half-moon-shaped pastry. Trim off any excess dough, leaving a ½-inch edge around the filling, and crimp the edges together with a fork to seal them. Transfer the pies to a parchment-lined baking sheet and refrigerate them for 30 minutes.

5. Preheat the vegetable oil in a deep fryer to 350°F. Line a baking sheet with paper towels and sprinkle sugar lightly over the paper towels.

6. Working in batches, fry the pies until golden brown on both sides, 4 to 5 minutes. As they are cooked, transfer them to the prepared baking sheet and sprinkle the tops of the pies with sugar. Serve the pies warm, with vanilla bean ice cream or whipped cream if desired.

Apple Fritters

These are light and tender on the inside and crisp, chewy, and cinnamon-sweet on the outside. Great on their own, but they sure would kick plain vanilla ice cream up a notch.

2 tablespoons unsalted butter
4 cups peeled and diced Fuji or Gala apples
    (¼-inch dice)
2 tablespoons light brown sugar
1 teaspoon ground cinnamon
Pinch of freshly grated nutmeg
Pinch of salt
2 eggs, separated
¾ cup apple cider
1 cup all-purpose flour
1 teaspoon baking powder
1 cup plus 1 tablespoon granulated sugar
Vegetable oil, for deep-frying

1. Melt the butter in a 12-inch skillet over medium-high heat. Add the apples and sauté, stirring frequently, for 2 minutes. Sprinkle in the brown sugar, ¼ teaspoon of the cinnamon, the nutmeg, and salt, and cook for 2 to 3 minutes more, until the apples are lightly coated with the syrup. Remove the skillet from the heat and set aside to cool.

2. In a medium bowl, whisk together the egg yolks and apple cider. Stir in the cooled apple mixture.

3. In a large bowl, combine the flour, baking powder, and the 1 tablespoon granulated sugar. Make a well in the center of the flour and add the apple mixture. Gradually incorporate the flour into the wet ingredients, mixing gently with a whisk until uniform. Set the batter aside for 20 minutes.

4. Preheat the vegetable oil in a deep fryer to 350°F. Set a wire rack over a paper-towel-lined baking sheet.

5. Using an electric hand mixer, whip the egg whites until soft peaks form. Gently fold the whites into the batter until completely blended.

6. In a medium bowl, combine the remaining 1 cup sugar with the remaining ¾ teaspoon cinnamon. Set aside half of this mixture in a medium container for the final sprinkling.

7. Working in batches of 3 or 4, and being careful not to overcrowd the fryer, add 2-tablespoon scoops of the fritter batter to the fryer. Fry the fritters for 4 to 5 minutes, until golden and cooked through, turning them as needed for even color. Remove the fritters with a slotted spoon or strainer, drain briefly, toss them in the bowl of cinnamon sugar, and set them aside on the wire rack.

8. Once you have finished frying them, roll the fritters a final time in the reserved cinnamon sugar, or just sprinkle the cinnamon sugar over the top. Serve immediately.

Fried Bananas with Rum Caramel Sauce

Store-bought spring roll wrappers make this dessert a breeze to throw together. Wonton wrappers will work, too, but I find the spring roll wrappers fry up extra-crispy. If you like, you can make the Rum Caramel Sauce as much as several weeks ahead. Warning: the sauce is addictively good on just about anything!

Vegetable oil, for deep-frying
12 large spring roll wrappers
3 firm-ripe bananas, halved lengthwise and
   then crosswise to make 12 pieces total
¾ cup packed light or dark brown sugar
1 egg, lightly beaten
Vanilla ice cream, for serving
Rum Caramel Sauce (recipe follows),
   for serving
Chopped toffee candy bars (such as Heath),
   for garnish

1. Preheat the vegetable oil in a deep fryer to 375°F. Position a wire rack over a paper-towel-lined baking sheet.

2. On a clean work surface and working in small batches, position a few spring roll wrappers so that one point faces to the bottom (they will look like diamonds). Place 1 piece of banana in the center of each wrapper so that it sits perpendicular to the two side corners. Top each piece of banana with 1 tablespoon of the brown sugar. Using a brush, lightly moisten the edges of the wrappers with the beaten egg. Fold the bottom corner of each wrapper up and over the banana, and then fold the two side corners over the banana. Finally, roll the banana up, egg roll fashion, so that it is fully enclosed, and press the edges together to secure them.

3. Working in batches, fry the bananas until crisp and golden brown on all sides, 3 to 4 minutes. Transfer them to the wire rack to drain briefly. Cut each fried banana in half diagonally and arrange 4 pieces in each dessert bowl. Top with a scoop of vanilla ice cream and drizzle liberally with the Rum Caramel Sauce. Garnish with the chopped toffee candy bars, to taste.

Rum Caramel Sauce About 1¾ cups

1 cup sugar
¼ cup hot water
1 cup plus 1 tablespoon heavy cream
2 tablespoons dark rum
1 teaspoon vanilla extract
2 teaspoons cold unsalted butter
Pinch of salt

Combine the sugar and hot water in a heavy saucepan, and cook over high heat until the sugar has dissolved, about 1 minute. Continue to cook, swirling the pan occasionally but never stirring the mixture, until it thickens and turns a deep amber color, 5 to 8 minutes. Remove the saucepan from the heat and add the heavy cream; be careful, the mixture will splatter. Return the pan to the heat and reduce the heat to medium-low. Cook until the sauce is thick and creamy, stirring occasionally to help the caramel melt into the cream, about 5 minutes. Remove from the heat and stir in the rum, vanilla, butter, and salt. Serve warm.

NOTE: *The sauce can be made up to 2 weeks in advance and refrigerated in an airtight container. Rewarm it gently before serving.*

Acknowledgments

As always, many people play a part in helping me bring a new book to life. My sincerest thanks go to:

My family: Alden, EJ, Meril, Jessie, Jilly, Mom, Dad, Mark, Wendi, Katti Lynn, Dolores, Jason, Jude, John Peter, and Steven.

My culinary team: Charlotte Martory, Alain Joseph, Stacey Meyer, and Kamili Hemphill.

My Homebase team: Eric Linquest, Tony Cruz, Dave McCelvey, Chef Chris Wilson, Chef Bernard Carmouche, Tony Lott, George Ditta, Maggie McCabe, and Camille Breland. Plus all of the dedicated employees at Homebase and at each of my restaurants.

Photographers Chris Granger and Colin Lacy.

My Martha Stewart Living Omnimedia associates: Martha Stewart, Ken West, Dan Taitz, Lucinda Scala Quinn, and Sarah Carey.

Michelle Terrebonne, Paige Capossela Green, Julia Howles, and Melanie Summers.

My associates at William Morrow/HarperCollins: Cassie Jones, Kara Zauberman, Liate Stehlik, Lynn Grady, Tavia Kowalchuk, Lauren Cook, Shawn Nicholls, Joyce Wong, Ann Cahn, Kathie Ness, Leah Carlson-Stanisic, and Karen Lumley.

My partners: B&G Foods, Green Mountain Coffee Roasters Inc., Groupe SEB/T-Fal, New Orleans Fish House, Nuovo Pasta, and SED International, La Collina, Lenox/Gorham, White Coffee & World Kitchen, William Morris Endeavor Entertainment.

Index